MARKETING CONVERGENCE

How the Leading Companies Are Profiting from Integrating Online and Offline Marketing Strategies

SUSAN K. JONES
Ferris State University
The Callahan Group, PLC

TED SPIEGEL
Northwestern University
Spiegel Marketing Associates

RĀCOM
COMMUNICATIONS

THOMSON

Australia · Canada · Mexico · Singapore · Spain · United Kingdom · United States

THOMSON
™

Marketing Convergence: How the Leading Companies Are Profiting from Integrating Online and Offline Markeing Strategies
By Susan K. Jones and Ted Spiegel

Editor-in-Chief
Jack Calhoun

Vice President/
Executive Publisher
Dave Shaut

Acquisition Editor
Steve Momper

Cunsulting Editor in
Marketing
Richard Hagle

Channel Manager,
Professional
Mark Linton

Production Manager
Tricia Matthews Boies

Production Editor
Alan Biondi

Manufacturing
Coordinator
Charlene Taylor

Compositor
Sans Serif Inc.

Cover Design
Anne Marie Rekow

Printer
Phoenix Book Technology
Hagerstown, MD

ISBN: 0-538-72719-5

For Cindy Sue and Louis XIV

Contents

CONTENTS

Foreword

It's hard not to play Monday morning quarterback when reflecting upon the recent dot.com phenomenon. The rush to gain leverage in the new economy has led some of the most experienced marketers to ignore tried-and-true marketing principles. Blinded by the Internet's promise for quantum growth and lucrative IPOs, many companies wandered off the straight-and-narrow and into a new world fraught with little more than broken dreams.

As marketers who truly believe in the power of brand equity and customer loyalty, shouldn't we have known that launching independent, ground-up Web-based businesses would be less successful than integrating this new medium as an extension of an existing brand's footprint? Wouldn't it have been prudent to expect delays in consumer adoption of new technologies and behaviors? Couldn't we have predicted that the market forces governing capitalism would eventually correct inflated stock prices? Granted, there will always be room for the innovator with a truly breakthrough business proposition to succeed. However, after the dust settled, very few success stories have emerged from the "dot.bomb" rubble.

Given the feeding frenzy around going online in most industries a few years ago, the question was not *if* launching an Internet play was appropriate, but *when* and *how*. Most companies believed they had to dive into the game with both feet to keep from being passed by. Why not chance breakthrough success? The problem was they ignored the rules of the game . . . the rules that marketers have practiced for years. And in the end, many learned the lesson we now see so clearly.

To the consumer with existing brand loyalties, each brand interaction must be integrated and seamless with the last. Consumers tend not to distinguish between media and channels within a brand franchise, but rather view their relationship with a company holistically. While each medium has its own characteristics, especially those uniquely inherent in the Web, they must be considered part and parcel to the overall brand experience. Hence, *Marketing Convergence.*

Blending their collective wisdom from years of business and academic experience, authors Ted Spiegel and Susan K. Jones uncover recent case studies highlighting successful attempts at achieving marketing convergence. Companies represented span across industries and are both large and small, well known and unfamiliar. The authors demonstrate the proven success factors that set the stage for successful integration of the Internet into the overall customer experience.

Not surprising is that some of those success factors look strangely familiar to marketing practices proven true in the old economy. Leveraging brand equity. Evolving with changing consumer needs. Blending high tech with high touch. Building profitable customer relationships. And the newly evident point: the Internet is best approached from a direct marketing frame of reference, where everything can be tested and measured in light of its impact on customer behavior and loyalty. Case in point, catalog marketers have been some of the most profitable and successful in integrating on-line marketing into its existing business practices, as noted in this book.

Also of interest are some of the points about how the Internet, while part of the whole brand message, does truly have unique capabilities and can reach the consumer in new and compelling ways. How its information gathering usage and video/audio capabilities can be utilized to make the consumer experience more in-depth and engaging. How real-time marketing changes the competitive game. How increased consumer access enhances customer retention.

So, admit it. While it might be easy to play Monday morning quarterback, didn't you find yourself caught up in the same excitement? Our view of the Internet is more grounded now, but it is still very much an exciting place, yet to be harnessed to its full potential. Through the lessons of the past few years, perhaps you have developed more conviction about what the right course for the Internet is at your company today. The fact is, even though it looks a little different than what we had originally thought, the Web is here to stay.

The case studies contained in the following pages will surely sharpen your understanding of how to make the Internet, in its current state, work harder for you and your consumer. The complexities are great to truly achieve marketing convergence, but your business will benefit greatly for your trying.

Good luck as you follow the course to convergence!

CLAIRE BRAND, General Manager, Hallmark Keepsake Ornaments
SCOTT ROBINETTE, President, Hallmark Loyalty Marketing Group

Co-authors of: *Emotion Marketing: The Hallmark Way of Winning Customers for Life*

Preface

Although the word *convergence* has appeared in English dictionaries since 1713, the term has taken on an almost mystical significance in 21st-century parlance. For scientists, politicians, IT professionals, communicators and marketers, *convergence* resonates with possibilities, contexts and meanings.

- An article in the November 2000 issue of *Scientific American* magazine, "Creating *Convergence*," examines what it will take to "achieve the union of audio, video, and data communications into a single source, received on a single device, delivered by a single connection."
- The Nanobiotechnology Center at Cornell University is devoted to "studying the *convergence* of nano-microfabrication and biosystems."
- The Norman Lear Center at the University of Southern California bills itself as "a multi-disciplinary research and public policy center exploring implications of the *convergence* of entertainment, commerce, and society."
- Key:Cat and :CueCat devices promise the *convergence* of the print and interactive worlds. By reading codes on the pages of magazines, books or other print media, these hand-held gizmos "serve as a precise bridge connecting your printed materials to specific pages deep within the Internet."
- Satirist Phil Patiris of moderntv.com laments the *convergence* of news and entertainment on network television beginning with the Gulf War and continuing with other military campaigns in the Middle East.
- A trade newspaper called *Restructuring Today* focuses on "retail gas and electric competition, electric and gas utility restructuring, *convergence*, and deregulation."

- As part of a 2001 May Day celebration, a political group held "Carnival Against Capitalism," billed as an anticapitalist *convergence* in Quebec City, Quebec, Canada.

Merriam-Webster's says that *the act of converging* coordinates "the movement of the two eyes so that the image of a single point is formed on corresponding retinal areas." But an alternate meaning stresses the "independent development of similar characters . . . often associated with similarity of habits or environment." So what does *convergence* mean to us as marketers today? Coming together? Streamlining? Working in sync? Or does *convergence* somehow promote a result that's greater than the sum of its parts?

In the early 1990s, marketers spoke hopefully about the forthcoming *convergence* of television, computer and telephone as envisioned in the *Scientific American* article noted above. This idealistic concept met with defeat after agonizing defeat as cable television, telephone and computer firms failed to come to terms for their planned mergers and acquisitions. The monolith known as AOL Time Warner now strives to make this form of *convergence* a reality—and, even with their recent problems, they probably stand a better chance than most. Meanwhile, software giant Microsoft continues to hedge its bets by investing in both interactive television and computer applications.

The Meaning of Marketing Convergence

While a true union of the TV, phone and computer remains a somewhat elusive goal, a number of sophisticated companies have already scored significant successes with *marketing convergence*. This term refers to the orchestration of Information Technology, Marketing and Design required to ensure that companies present an integrated, consistent, clear and interactive message across all the media they use. Today's efforts at *marketing convergence* are fueled by the growth of the Internet and the World Wide Web, but *marketing convergence* is complicated by the fact that the Internet represents so much more than "just another medium to add to the mix." For example:

- The Internet allows for targeting very specific groups and individuals, making one-to-one marketing a reality.
- The Internet allows marketers to cultivate true, real-time conversations with their customers rather than one-way messages or delayed communications.
- The Internet allows for unprecedented depth of information, product assortment, and personalization—even modification "on the fly" to deal with a customer's wishes.
- The Internet represents a new challenge in that instead of merely "pushing" media messages to customers and prospects, it requires that customers be attracted to the Web site. Once there, they are not confined by a linear message but must be attracted to "dig deeper."

To find out how smart marketers are meeting the challenges of *marketing convergence*, we performed extensive interviews with 23 top marketing and e-commerce executives at more than a dozen companies throughout the United States. We then synthesized the results of these interviews to determine *nine vital areas of focus* that companies must master in order to maximize their success both online and offline. We also produced a short case history on each company we visited, focused on that firm's most vital "lessons learned" in its first months or years of Internet marketing.

The resulting book, *Marketing Convergence,* shows how direct and interactive marketers today are wrestling with the challenges of integrating interactive media with their traditional promotional and selling methods such as space and broadcast advertising, direct mail, catalogs and retail outlets. It also shares the secrets of several unusually successful firms that have invented or re-invented themselves with the Internet at the center of their businesses.

SUSAN K. JONES
EDWARD J. SPIEGEL
July 2002

Acknowledgments

A number of individuals have been extremely helpful in the research and writing of this book. They include:

- Ed Bjorncrantz, our partner in The Callhan Group, LLC, who acted as the "test case" for book interviewing when he was still at J. C. Whitney. Ed also was instrumental in securing and conducting our interview at Carnival Cruise Lines.
- Brent Gledhill of William Blair & Company, LLC/London office, who made the introductions that secured our interview at Action Performance.
- Terry Kelly of BDO Seidman, LLP, for his kind cooperation in expediting approval of the Mindpepper/bargainandhaggle.com materials.
- All of our 23 interviewees, listed at the end of the book, for their investment of time and their refreshing candor.
- Our editor and publisher, Rich Hagle of RACOM Communications, for envisioning this project, for his belief in us as authors, and for all of his contributions and investments in *Marketing Convergence*.

Our sincere thanks and appreciation to you all.

I | *The Strategies*

1 | Does the Internet Change Everything?

Most marketing and IT conferences circa 1997–2000 featured at least one keynoter asserting, "The Internet Changes Everything." Gurus like Christopher Locke (*The Cluetrain Manifesto*) and Seth Godin (*Permission Marketing*) made the rounds of the marketing shows with their mystical pronouncements about "markets as conversations" and "avoiding interruption advertising." During that idealistic time period, speakers and authors in many other fields made similar provocative declarations of their own.

- Mercer University School of Law Professor Stephen M. Johnson contended that "The Internet Changes Everything" in public participation and access to government information.
- As General Counsel for the New Jersey Conference of Mayors, Andrew Weber predicted that more and more tax liens would be sold at auction since tracking down uncollected property taxes online is so much easier than tracking them by traditional methods.

- Showing a picture of a computer preparing to hungrily devour a telephone, Dr. Tim Kelly of the International Telecommunications Union quoted Eric Schmidt of Novell saying, "We started out running the 'Net on top of the phone system, and we'll end up with telephony running over the 'Net."

Yet as dot.coms died and the promise of swift and radical transformation to e-business faded like the Nasdaq's all-time high of 5,132.52, many executives exhibited a more jaded perspective. Indeed, a study by A. T. Kearney and Line 56 said, according to *iMarketing News* online for December 19, 2001, "While the overwhelming majority of companies plan to launch new Internet business projects in 2002, *top brass wants nothing to do with initiatives that will 'transform' their companies or industries.* Instead, CEOs want *measurable value and return on investment* in new Internet initiatives, the survey of 259 e-business executives determined."

Now that marketers realize the Internet is more likely to serve as a valuable vehicle rather than a "total transformation," they're able to step back and deal realistically with its plusses and minuses. Many conservative firms start with the concrete notion that the Internet is "just another channel." Then they may develop it as a unique and profitable marketing method, to the extent that it enhances their relationships with customers and prospects. And for some marketing organizations—but not all—the Internet *may* turn out to represent a whole new way of doing business.

Marketers Recognize the Internet's Many Strengths

Even if the Internet isn't going to completely transfigure the marketing world as some once thought, it does have a number of outstanding attributes for direct and interactive marketers. The "plusses" most-often mentioned by executives interviewed include:

- Research resource for buyers, sellers and learners:
  —"The Internet provides an ability for the consumer to learn more about the options that are available to them. It provides an opportunity to overcome objections and concerns."
  —Diana Rodriguez-Velazquez, Carnival Cruise Lines
  —"The Internet is now the quick research resource for many people about specific things they want to know. You get online, you get the answer, and you leave."
  —Glenda Plummer, Yamaha Band and Orchestral Division
- Elevates and extends strong existing brands:
  —"If you have a brand, acquisition costs online are low. If you don't have a brand, acquisition costs are extremely high. If you start with a well-known brand, people will search for your name as well as for terms related to what you sell. They will search for the brand 'J.C. Whitney' more than they will for terms like car parts, truck parts, auto parts."
  —Ed Bjorncrantz, formerly of J.C. Whitney
  —"The Internet provides a great arena for extending your brand. Some people have the perception that if you don't plan on selling anything, you shouldn't even have a Web site. It's expensive, and so on. But today when you hear about a company, the first thing people ask is, 'what's their Web site?'"
  —Jim Shanks, CDW
- Cost-effective for self-service and ongoing business:
  —"Site visitors can answer questions for themselves without having to ask on the phone."
  —Kevin Giglinto, Chicago Symphony Orchestra
  —"While the start-up cost is high, the cost of doing business once you have your platform in place is relatively low, especially versus catalog with the variable expense of production. Online you have a lot of fixed costs up front. If you can gener-

ate traffic, your variable cost of doing business is relatively low."

—Ed Bjorncrantz, formerly of J.C. Whitney

- Allows for unprecedented one-to-one communications and dynamic personalization on the fly:

  —"The Internet is the first one-to-one marketing avenue that's dynamic and customizable. People can tailor the site to see what they want to see and the organization behind the site can look at their behaviors and tailor to that as well."

  —Jim Shanks, CDW

  —"When you log into our site it knows who you are and what needs to be done—how many completed deals you have yet to rate, and so on. We recommend categories based on your past shopping with our suggestion tool."

  —Catherine Ettinger, formerly of Mindpepper

- Opens the market to new groups of customers:

  —"The person who shops online might never go into your store—they have a different psyche than the retail shopper. They seem like the same customer who calls the toll-free number—demographics, education, household value—but actually they're a whole different animal, motivated by different things."

  —Steve Katzman, American Blind and Wallpaper Factory

  —Spiegel, Chicago Symphony Orchestra, Quixtar, Omaha Steaks and American Blind and Wallpaper Factory all report that their online customers are younger than their offline customers, which bodes well for their long-term value.

- Powerful Extranets customize to the company and individual:

  —"Steelcase's approach has never been 'one size fits all.' Ensync, which is our e-business platform, is designed to provide customized solutions for our customers. Whether it's access to customer specific information, access to tailored product and service catalogs, ability to review online standards/mark up active CAD drawings/keep updated via project folders or providing the option to access inventory that the customer already owns, we provide solutions that are capable of meeting each customer's specific needs. Steelcase's advantage is its ability to provide this capability through the seamless integration of a group of eTools which—when working together—provide the customer with a single integrated solution. You don't have to step out of one tool to another with different passwords. 'One door—one entry.'"

—Jeff Vredevoogd, Steelcase Inc.

—"Whether you are a new customer or an old customer, you can have a customized Extranet that you can use for years to see your whole purchase history. Also, the Extranet takes it beyond sales to customer service. Customers can do purchase history downloads, asset tagging, returns authorization, order status, freight tracking, and accounting systems to look at open invoices, payments and aging on their accounts."

—Jim Shanks, CDW

- Unlimited real estate so prospects can dig deeper and marketers can present items that wouldn't pay out in print:
  - —"At a trade show there is only so much real estate even if you have a lot of handouts. But with the Web site you have unlimited real estate. Prospects can look at who the officers are for credibility, and check for financial stability and press releases, as well as products and background."

    —Jim Shanks, CDW

  - —"In the J.C. Whitney print catalog there are 55,000 SKUs; on Internet there are 100,000 additional products that could never be listed cost-effectively in the catalog. The incremental cost of listing products online is low. When J.C. Whitney went online, they also extended the product line in custom areas."

    —Ed Bjorncrantz, formerly of J.C. Whitney

- Allows for profitable strategic alliances and affiliations:
  - —According to Dave Martin, Action Performance's strategic alliance with QVC to create www.qvc.com/goracing.html provided a "win-win" for these firms. Action Performance married its wealth of exclusively licensed NASCAR col-

lectibles products with QVC's huge audience, infrastructure and fulfillment capabilities.

—"Quixtar is either the number-one or number-two affiliate partner for many of the companies that appears on its site. (These include Omaha Steaks, Disney Store, KBToys, and OfficeMax.) Partner sites are tested for several months before they are approved. Some don't past the test. They must keep track by Independent Business Owner number so the proper IBO gets credit for the sale. You are always framed in the Quixtar site when you go to affiliate sites."

—Ken McDonald, Quixtar

- Offers unique ways to present information and increase sales and profits:

—Omaha Steaks avoids distracting customers with affiliate offers while they're in the active part of the firm's Web site. Affiliate links are revealed only after the customer buys, on the thank-you page.

—CDW offers side-by-side comparisons of computers for prospective buyers with high levels of detail

—American Blind and Wallpaper is perfecting an amazon.com-like system by which the site will tell buyers "people who have purchased this item have also purchased these complementary items"—thereby encouraging larger average order sizes

High-Volume Targeted E-Mails at Very Low Cost

In addition to these oft-heard benefits, the 'Net has brought marketers at least one particularly valuable dividend. Marketers now send millions of targeted, opted-in e-mails per year at a tiny fraction of the cost of direct mail or phone.

Using the relatively easy, inexpensive medium of outgoing e-mail responsibly is a mandate for every online marketer. And with their proclivity for constant testing, sophisticated e-commerce companies learn quickly what works and what doesn't in the e-mail realm.

Spiegel sent out 58 million targeted e-mail messages during 2001, according to Rich Burke. "It's our lowest cost-per-action advertising vehicle," he says. "We carefully track the ratio of e-mails received to orders placed. We're just beginning to do segmentation on our e-mails, collecting data from our buyers. Personalization makes more sense to me on e-mail than it does on the site. It's 'one to a few' marketing. We base personalization on your buying history, not on what some computer thinks you might buy in the future."

Quixtar uses e-mail to communicate with its Independent Business Owners (IBOs), according to John Parker. "We have information about our IBOs that we utilize in how we communicate with them. We send out about 150,000 targeted e-mails a month, but they are very specifically pointed with a message that will have meaning to those folks. It's easier to execute that personalization on the Web than it is in a printed catalog."

Omaha Steaks has an e-mail file of a couple of million names, "but only about 250,000 buyers," says Todd Simon. "We have a lot of inquiries. All of the two million names are opted in. We e-mail to them about every two weeks."

Peapod currently offers an opt-in "weekly specials" e-mail that about 65 percent of its customers receive. "We also have a referral service that works via e-mail," Parkinson says. "If you get a friend to join, you get $20 when they put in the code."

CDW has a subscription newsletter, *CDW Buyers' Edge*. "We tell them about the latest product offerings as well as ways to get the most from our Web site, and so on," Shanks notes. "Our *Buyer's Edge* newsletter is published during the first part of the week," he adds. There are several different versions of the newsletter based on customer preferences and interests.

The preceding has been just a brief outline of some of the exciting marketing possibilities brought about by the Internet. Chapters 1 through 9 are devoted to the key strategies that the most successful thought leaders and practitioners are using to integrate online and offline efforts for greater profitability. Chapters 10 through 22 offer individual case histories based on the baker's dozen of companies studied. Others will no doubt emerge as the new electronic media continue to evolve, but these are the strategies that are working today—and are likely to be the base of the new breakthroughs of tomorrow.

Chapter Recap:

- The Internet is no longer considered "transformational."
- Today's Internet initiatives must pull their own weight.
- Executives recognize significant current drawbacks to online marketing:
  —Open for all to see unless password protected.
  —Potential for channel conflict.
  —Small, predatory firms may do significant damage to brands.
  —Poor tracking standards to date.
  —Selling methods not yet optimized online.
- Online marketing also offers significant current benefits:
  —Research resource for buyers, sellers and learners.
  —Elevates and extends strong, existing brands.
  —Cost-effective for self-service and repeat business.
  —One-to-one and on-the-fly personalization.
  —Powerful Extranets.
  —Unlimited real estate.
  —Strategic alliances and affiliations.
  —Unique and profitable new ways to present information.
- E-mail represents a high-volume, targeted medium available at very low cost.

2 | Who Survived the Dot.com Bomb— and Why

Visit www.disobey.com/ghostsites/, and you can buy a colorful "Museum of E-Failure" mouse pad emblazoned with the logos of almost-famous, now-dead "dot.bombs." Or pick up a T-shirt bearing the telltale death knell online message, "This page cannot be displayed." The site also features hundreds of farewell screen shots salvaged for posterity from dead dot.coms, including high-profile failures such as etoys.com, webvan.com, and weddingchannel.com.

As the disobey.com site's creator, Stephen Baldwin, explains, "This exhibit—the Museum of E-Failure (aka Ghost Sites of the Web)—is one person's attempt to actively preserve some relics from the Great Web Boom, a long-ago period of frenetic activity spanning the years 1998 and 2001. Our goal is not to laugh at these failed enterprises, but to preserve some high-quality documentary images (complete with classic banner ads and zeitgeist-laden editorial content)—as many as possible. These sites served us well—they may be gone, but they should not be forgotten—not yet, anyway." By the end of 2001 Baldwin had harvested over 900 defunct site images and vowed to keep on at least until he had an even 1,000 companies in his online "museum."

Meanwhile, a site called f***edcompany.com offers profane-yet-timely news of the latest dot.com failures—and boasts an Amazon.com affiliate banner at the top of its welcome page. Planet-pinkslip.com features unemployment humor, Pink Slip Party advice, job resources, t-shirts, e-sympathy cards, dot.com bomb news and more "for the laid off, fired, downsized, rightsized or otherwise unemployed victims of the New Economy." On the bright side (for all except those who made a living running this site), thecompost.com officially ceased publication on September 12, 2001 "due to a severe slowdown in dot.com demise." Thecompost.com had devoted itself exclusively to "tracking the death of the dot.com."

Throwing Cold Water on "Internet Ecstasy"

Today it's much harder than it used to be to gain an audience for rhapsodies about the Internet's revolutionary properties. Indeed, many top marketers now view the medium with unblinking realism and candor. "It's high-speed direct marketing—that's all!" says Rich Burke of Spiegel. "It's not that much different for our company than the last 135 years." Notes Todd Simon of Omaha Steaks, "It's a new front-end on an existing business—it's not Internet retailing—it's retailing on the Internet." And Steve Katzman of American Blind and Wallpaper Factory calls online marketing "just another add-on channel of communication and distribution. Every time we've gone to a new way of selling, we've had a big bump in business. Getting one on the Internet is nothing out of the ordinary."

Seasoned marketers also realize the new channel has liabilities attached to it—just as all other emerging media have had in the past. Glenda Plummer of Yamaha Band and Orchestral Division points out the problems of providing targeted messages in a medium that's open to anyone, anywhere in the world. Jennifer Jurgens, formerly of Mindpepper, agrees. "You might think you are speaking to your target market, but you're really speaking to anyone and everyone. You have the potential to offend, and not much control of who sees your message."

Plummer says that for many firms selling business-to-business, the Internet is fraught with channel problems. "We'd like to sell a lot of things direct on the 'Net but our dealers stop us from thinking about it." Her colleague Gary Winder adds that so far Yamaha has only been able to sell "things the dealers don't want to deal with, like videos."

While the dealers watch Yamaha like a hawk, Winder says that the firm has had to become vigilant in monitoring its dealers' online activities as well. And since upstarts with good HTML skills can look very sophisticated online, it's difficult for consumers to tell legitimate dealers from pretenders. He explains, "Kitchen table-type dealers try to sell on price online. Some small dealers might buy only 10 items but on the Internet they can make it look like they stock a full line in-depth. To become a bona fide Yamaha e-commerce dealer the standard stocking has to be about $250,000 in inventory. A majority of our dealers are not sophisticated enough online to compete with the price-based shops. So now we are enforcing our Minimum Advertising Price Policy (MAPP) and if a dealer violates it they will lose all rights to buy from Yamaha." Glenda Plummer adds, "Otherwise it's unfair to dealers who do step up to the plate and stock a lot of product. MAPP also stops the dealers from being 'stupidly reactive' to price challenges and helps them support a price level."

Jennifer Jurgens laments the fact that the Internet is still a medium in its infancy and that "there aren't any standards for tracking. It differs company by company. How did this campaign really do? We're not 100 percent sure." Former Mindpepper CEO Catherine Ettinger says, "There's a fear factor that you can't quantify things. The press goes crazy about fraud aspects online and that comes back to haunt companies like ours. Being on the Internet ties your brand to the 'branding of the Internet.'" And like other direct marketing methods, the press and many consumers tend to judge the entire industry by its least responsible members.

Steve Katzman notes that, for his firm, conversion rates online are 35 percent less than they are on the phone. "With the customer in control, you can't take charge of selling," he says. "You don't have the ability to ask for a sale like you would at retail or on the phone, and you don't have the opportunity to figure out the customer's objection and overcome it. It's frustrating not to be able to answer simple questions like 'Do you take American Express.?' Even if it's all over the Web site—they may have missed it. But one of the reasons the customer comes to us online is that she likes that anonymity."

New Priorities in the New Economy

During 2000 and 2001, hundreds of "half-MBAs" rethought their rash decisions to abandon their studies for dot.com "sure riches" through stock options. Thousands more young workers hustled "B-to-B" (back to banking) or "B-to-C" (back to consulting) after watching their on-paper dot.com millionaire status wither to nothing. The media enjoyed a bonanza both during and after the dot.com heyday. First business and financial pundits built the dot.com boom to mythical status, and then they lamented the "death of the New Economy" in gloom-and-doom articles and televised reports.

Yet during this same time period, thousands of North American businesses quietly perfected their own online presences and started new units focused on Internet marketing. Projections for employment in e-commerce continue very strong, according to WEFA Group reports commissioned by the Direct Marketing Association. So how are these online businesses succeeding in the same atmosphere where hundreds of well-funded dot.coms failed miserably?

First, successful Internet marketers see the 'Net as an enhancement to traditional methods of doing business—not an apocalyptic marketing revolution. Second, they don't forget their basic "lessons learned" about how advertising and marketing work. Third, they know that leveraging a strong, well-established brand greatly diminishes the time and money required to start making money online. Fourth, they keep their investments in line with expected return. And, fifth, they don't hire IT "hotshots" or flashy outside vendors, but seek low-key talent locally or grow it from within.

Getting Real About Internet Marketing

Seventeen Web-related companies bought spots on Super Bowl 2000, bidding up the price to an unprecedented $2.5 million or more for each 30-second spot—and causing a number of Old Economy brands to seek more cost-effective advertising vehicles. Of those 17 New Economy firms, 7 were out of business before the end of the year 2000. And by the time Super Bowl 2001 rolled around, only 3 Internet companies—E-Trade, Monster.com and Hotjobs.com—were willing to fork over the cash for a spot. The same 3 plus Yahoo showed up on Super Bowl 2002, when spots dipped below $2 million per

30 seconds. Autotrader.com, a prominent Super Bowl advertiser in 2000, pulled back the following year in favor of an array of less pricey sporting events.

Classically trained marketers shook their heads in disbelief as the dot.com upstarts insisted that one or two Super Bowl spots could win them the brand recognition and sustained site traffic necessary to keep them in the limelight all year. These veterans calculated what they could do with $2.5 million in an integrated, highly segmented campaign of direct marketing, public relations, sales promotion and general advertising. Meanwhile, the "dot.com whippersnappers" scoffed at traditional "reach × frequency = gross rating points" media planning and rolled the dice for one big score.

The dot.com marketers did have at least one good point. Most of their firms began their lives with absolutely no brand recognition, and they realized that a mass medium like television could help them build the awareness they needed. But as 2000 and 2001 progressed, many dot.coms seemed to be fighting a losing battle. They faced formidable competitors with solid funding, long-established brand names and intuitive URLs that most prospects could key into their browsers without even looking them up. Some dot.com executives and their disillusioned venture capitalists finally realized that the Internet is simply a complement and supplement to a strong business, not a substitute.

Strong Brands Do Well Online

Many established companies have found that all they had to do was put up a Web site to experience a great deal of immediate traffic, based on their strong brand names. When Yamaha went online with its worldwide site, it attracted a quick build-up of traffic that has sustained over time, according to Glenda Plummer. "The Yamaha name is among the top 30 most recognizable brands in the world," she says. "Yamaha's corporate Web page gets over two million hits per month, in great part due to the strength of the name."

Rich Burke says that "for Spiegel, our brand is number-one online. The brand is probably more important on the Internet than in the catalog or retail stores because the 'Net is still new and unproven. People need to know they are working with a brand. They like that credibility. When we can get people to buy both online and offline, it doubles their value to us. The catalog is the key to that jump in value and volume—we get the names *Spiegel* and *Spiegel.com* in front of people 120 million times a year with catalog mailings." Burke also reveals that because of Spiegel's careful, step-by-step online investments and established brand, the firm has been profitable online from "day one."

Todd Simon of Omaha Steaks agrees with Burke's comments about credibility. He adds, "You can have a Web site for zero money, but you can't be in the catalog business for zero money. Brand plays an even bigger role on the Internet because of the level of uncertainty—consumers will gravitate toward a strong brand. There's not enough substance on the Internet alone. Our catalogs show customers our substance and investment, as do our retail stores."

Kevin Giglinto of the Chicago Symphony Orchestra has found that "people trust our brand, so they aren't afraid to put their credit card into our type of site. If you have an established brand you're in a better position—I never really have to worry about the brand while working with the symphony. The brand is highly regarded in Chicago because of the musicians. We also get a lot of store orders from Japan, Holland and Germany because the orchestra has played there frequently, thus strengthening the brand internationally."

Keep Online Investments
in Line with Expected Return

NASCAR collectibles marketer Action Performance is one company whose Web presence nearly drained its financial coffers and helped cause significant stock price erosion. But when Dave Martin came on the scene as Chief Financial Officer in late 2000, he applied his CPA standards to every dollar the firm invested from that day forward. As Martin explains, "I'm a 'belt and suspenders' kind of guy, so I hate to spend money. If we can't drive revenue through an expenditure, then I won't allocate the dollars. That simple reality wasn't focused on in the late 1990s because there were more grandiose things to think about with the dot.coms. But if you fully allocate your expenses and do what it takes to drive revenue, you *can* succeed online."

It may seem disingenuous for the executives of Quixtar to tout their frugality, considering the "deep pockets" of Alticor (parent company of Amway) that they have behind them. But they agree that it's important to focus expenditures in the right areas for long-term success online. As Ken McDonald stresses, "Hits don't count for profit, visitors don't count for profit, and amazon.com doesn't have enough profit to buy a laptop!" His colleague, John Parker, adds, "What created the bubble and burst was that companies started working for the wrong people—Wall Street and the stock price rather than building brands and the experience consumers want."

Mike Brennan of Peapod believes that for his firm, "Successes were often the things we didn't do. For instance, we had a chance to do one of those early $20 million portal deals with AOL, and we didn't do it, even though we were under serious pressure to do so. Peapod's Thomas Parkinson adds, "There was a lot of pressure in 1998 to raise some money to fund the business. Our investors said we should drop our relationship with retail grocers and be a pure-play dot.com company. But that's when our present owner, Ahold, stepped in to buy us. They're a $60 billion multinational company that has learned over the centuries how to let the locals run it. Click-and-brick is the right way to go to market for Peapod."

Now back on a conservative footing, Parkinson says of Peapod today, "I'm not in the business of being an evangelist for anybody's technology. When there is an installed base, I'm going to do it. The next one I'll take on is the Palm Pilot, but I'm not going to sell hardware or put scanners in your home." Brennan concurs, adding, "No kitchen of the future stuff."

Todd Simon thinks that Omaha Steaks' biggest success online has been that "we didn't over-think it at the beginning, but grew the business organically. We made a relatively small investment and learned as we went, then continued to build upon that learning. Other successes were actually all the mistakes we made which allowed us to 'back into' an excellent consumer experience on the Web. It's not like we went out and spent a million dollars and then had to do it all over. We grew it incrementally and cost-effectively."

Develop Your Own Systems and Talent In-House

Being "control freaks" where online systems and support are concerned seems to have paid off for many of the firms with successful and stable Web presences. As Rich Burke of Spiegel says, "We do it all internally. The only thing we don't do is host our own site. And we have an ad agency for banners, and an affiliate agency. If I can force a vendor to be on the cutting edge, it's better to be with them. Then I don't have to buy the newest, best equipment. There's certain expertise we just don't have. But we're actually pulling as much in-house as we can efficiently."

Steve Katzman at American Blind and Wallpaper Factory is amazed when he sees competitors like Sherwin-Williams turning over their Web presence to a third-party provider. "They do three billion dollars a year in sales, yet they're entrusting their online relationship with the customer to third parties." He says that Sherwin-Williams has begun offering custom-framed art through artselect.com. "It's artselect.com's back end that will do this. Sherwin-Williams is staking their brand on something with very little incremental revenue in proportion to the risk they are taking."

Most executives interviewed saw little difference in the job market for Web talent after the dot.com crash, since they either hire locally in towns like Omaha, Detroit, Phoenix or Grand Rapids—or train and grow their talent from within. In Chicago, however, Rich Burke finds that the employment climate has changed a great deal since the crash. "A couple of years ago we couldn't hire quality people; they wanted out-of-this world money. Now you can get quality people at affordable prices."

To the Victors Belong the Spoils

While many established firms found deep-pocket dot.coms to be annoying, if temporary, competitors, they now enjoy the opportunity to develop their own Web businesses in a less frenetic atmosphere. Ed Bjorncrantz comments on his former company: "J.C. Whitney is the leader in automotive parts and accessories on the Internet. Its two major competitors, carparts.com and wrenchhead.com, have gone out of business. They both had business models that didn't work. They burned through a lot of venture capital, didn't have the back end to support it, and 'lost money on every order, then tried to make it up on volume.'"

Glenda Plummer of Yamaha says that the death of some upstart dot.coms now lets larger firms develop their Web presence almost at leisure. "Most of our traditional competitors are way behind us on-line; we don't feel pushed at this point."

Peapod found the now-defunct webvan.com to be "a dumb competitor with money, like an airline offering $19 tickets to Florida," according to Mike Brennan. "Webvan went to half-hour delivery windows and offered 30,000 products, but we realized we couldn't do that profitably. We have two-hour delivery windows and 10,000 products. We cover what most people buy but couldn't make money offering the diversity of products that Webvan did. What we did wasn't sexy but our trucks are still in the street. We re-mained rational."

Randy Bancino of Quixtar explains why his firm has been able to grow rapidly in the face of the dot.com bust:

> Right now we're in that unfortunate but predictable part of the life-cycle curve. The whole Internet industry got over-hyped and now we are in the backlash period where we figure every idea from that era must have been a dumb idea. At Quixtar we didn't buy into that hype but stuck to our good fundamental business model and wove lots of cool technology stuff into that. The failed companies became too enamored with what they *could* do instead of looking at what they *should* do. I do think the industry will come out of that trough. Until then, smart companies will pick and choose what works.

At one time—in the early days of the automobile industry—there were more than 3,000 automobile manufacturers in the United States. That occurrence, coupled by many similar ones throughout the 20th century, should cause no surprise about the natural consolidation that has taken place in dot.coms and Internet-related businesses generally. Add to that the absence of sound marketing, integration, and business strategies, and the outcome should be seen as inevitable.

From this point on, we'll examine the strategies that will help you avoid the problems of the past and put you in line with the future. And we'll know how smart companies are implementing these strategies for success.

Chapter Recap:

- The death of many dot.coms actually foreshadowed success online for many firms.
- Successful Internet marketers keep five precepts firmly in mind:
  —The 'Net is a marketing enhancement, not an apocalyptic revolution.
  —The basics of how advertising and marketing work do not change online.
  —Leveraging a strong, well-established brand lets firms make money online faster than establishing new brands.
  —Keep investments in line with expected return.
  —Seek low-key local talent or grow talent from within. Avoid "dot.com hotshots" and flashy outside vendors.

3 | Successful Convergence = Integration

"Start with the customer and work back to the brand." That has been the mantra of Don Schultz, Bob Lauterborn and (the late) Stan Tannenbaum in their classic book, *Integrated Marketing Communications* (NTC/Contemporary, 1993). The authors stress the importance of developing a marketing communications mix that suits the customer's habits and preferences rather than the whims of an advertising agency or media planner.

IMC experts also point out that customers are easily confused when companies present them with conflicting messages and "looks" in various media. The way to get the most "bang for the media buck," they counsel, is to deliver the same Big Idea with the same graphics and tone whether you're designing a retail store or utilizing direct marketing, general advertising, sales promotion or public relations. As the IMC concept has evolved, it also has increased its focus on one-to-one communications between buyer and seller—necessitating a sophisticated database integrated across all media.

Today the Internet has become a vital element in the marketing communications mix for most major firms. And Internet marketers who lose sight of the importance of integration with other channels and media will do so at their peril. So while some firms may choose to present a different message and "look" online, they must make that decision strategically. And most firms will be best served by presenting a Web site that harmonizes with the images and messages of their traditional print and broadcast media.

Integrated "Look and Feel"

For a simple example of "total integration," leaf through the print catalog of Tiffany & Co., then log on to their Web site at www.tiffany.com and then visit one of their elegant retail stores. Tiffany's catalogs almost always feature the same shiny robin's egg blue cover and white internal pages with minimal copy, lots of negative space (white space), and simple-yet-tasteful product presentation. The Web site displays those same colors, graphics and type styles, which you'll see echoed again at the retail store where every Tiffany's purchase is presented in a shiny robin's egg blue box with silky white ribbon.

Firms with a more diverse product line, media mix and customer profile than that of Tiffany's may need additional work on the back end to achieve such integration, but they usually find it's well worth the effort. According to Jim Shanks of CDW, this concept was considered so important that his firm created a Strategic Business Unit (SBU) for the Web site, "charged with staying integrated with the rest of the organization." The SBU members make sure that CDW and CDWG (the firm's governmental and educational arm) "use the same messaging and positioning on the Web site that are found in the company's offline media."

When quixtar.com was under development as a new Web-based business for Alticor (parent company of Amway), marketing executives gave the fledgling Web site its own extensive "persona," according to Quixtar's Ken McDonald and John Parker. While they won't reveal the Quixtar persona's full profile, McDonald did share a few tidbits aimed at helping his designers and writers deliver a consistent message both online and offline.

"We try to evoke a certain feeling," he explains. "If Quixtar were a person it would dress in bright, vibrant colors including green. Quixtar would Rollerblade, would volunteer for Habitat for Humanity, eat bagels, drink Starbucks coffee, enjoy classic rock and jazz, and watch 'Ed,' 'The West Wing' and 'The Sopranos' on TV." He adds that such indicators used to be called Creative Guidelines, but now have been re-named Creative Standards—"to make it tougher."

A Strategic Choice for a Unique Online Focus

As much as marketers value the customer knowledge and recognition they gain by integrating their messages, some firms decide to modify their "look and feel" online for corporate reasons. For example, Ed Bjorncrantz says that jcwhitney.com "has better product presentation and easier search" than the firm's catalogs. "It's definitely not just the J. C. Whitney catalog put up on the Web. "You can only 'cut' a catalog two-dimensionally—by vehicle, by product category, or some simple combination. But on the Web site you can do search by vehicle, key word, product, or any other method that's helpful to the customer. You are really trying to structure a Web site to allow the customer to navigate the way they want to do it. You can also create specialty 'landing pages' that help address certain markets that are attracted through e-mails, affiliate programs, banner ads and the like. But, on the other hand, J. C. Whitney is a pretty basic-looking site, and also a pretty basic-looking catalog. Neither has a lot of 'flash' or complex presentation."

Steve Katzman of American Blind and Wallpaper Factory says his online customer is "a different consumer who is motivated by different things." While the firm pushes price over service in most other media they use, "The online consumer is less price sensitive and more tuned in to service and selection. So you'll still see our print media 'scream' 85 percent off plus an extra 10 percent off in bright colors while online you'll see a focus on functionality, product selection and service with price mentioned secondarily."

Integrating the Database

On the other hand, Katzman is completely in accord with the concept of one integrated database that covers every transaction and communication, no matter what medium is involved. "We run our business as one big profit center, but we clearly identify the productivity of each type of medium down to the individual online banner, space ad and TV spot. We tag people all the way through, no matter what or how many media they utilize. We built our database in-house so we'd be able to monitor every request, action and sale."

At CDW the same is true. As Jim Shanks relates, "Our account managers can pull up an account and see in a summary system how many times that customer has used the Web site and/or their Extranet, what they've been buying, how many tech support calls have been made, what returns were made, sales this year versus last year, and much more. We have our own Customer Relationship Management system that we built in-house, and our own order management system. We like to build things!"

Spiegel has been very successful in integrating its call centers with its catalog and Internet channels, according to Rich Burke. "All three of our companies (Spiegel, Newport News and Eddie Bauer) send their Internet calls into the same center and there has been proper training for the customer service reps on how to deal with these calls as well as Web-generated e-mails," Burke reveals. "Working on the Internet business is a perk or privilege for our best reps."

Let the Customer Buy When and Where They Want

Most direct and interactive marketers agree that if they can entice a customer to buy both online and offline, that customer's long-term value will grow. Yet they also realize the best way to build satisfaction and loyalty is to cater to the customer's buying preferences and habits.

Spiegel does make an effort to get its online customers to buy offline and vice-versa, as Burke explains. "If you buy on the Web but have never bought via catalog, we circulate you very heavily. We also circulate Web offers to catalog-only buyers; that has been less than successful. Internet shoppers are very willing to shop the catalog but not vice-versa, and so far we don't know why. If we can get them to buy from both channels, their value to us doubles. We try not to make the channel choice for the customer—we say 'buy however you want to buy.' If we make a promotional offer in the catalog, it can be redeemed on the 'Net and vice-versa."

Steve Katzman agrees with Burke's philosophy, calling American Blind and Wallpaper Factory "the Burger King of the home decorating industry—have it your way! Whatever way you want to communicate with us, we'll do it. It costs too much to have a customer consider working with you to shut them down by not facilitating the buying channel they prefer."

Katzman and his staff also try to smooth the way for buyers through their online Personal Shopper program. "You describe what you are looking for and within 24 hours we respond with options to fit your needs. We process 1,000 of these each day for people who don't know how to use the site or just don't have time to figure it out. That's one-to-one marketing to the nth degree. We have people dedicated especially to these requests and they receive extra training."

Ed Bjorncrantz has found that offering multiple buying methods—in and of itself—stimulates more sales for J. C. Whitney. "The Internet generates catalog interest and vice-versa. Customers who use both are better customers. Customers can use the Internet to supplement what they learn from the catalog. You're wise to make it a similar customer experience. The customer looks at a brand somewhat monolithically. In my past experience at Sears, a synergy also existed between catalog and retail. People would shop the catalog and go to the retail store to touch, feel and buy. Or maybe they would look at an item in the store and go home and buy later from the catalog."

Ken McDonald of Quixtar says that in his business, "people don't shop online, they buy online," whereas for CDW it is the opposite. Shanks sees customers going online to make detailed comparisons among the computer models available, but then calling his firm's toll-free number for the reassurance of human contact in finalizing a big-ticket purchase. Only about 15 percent of CDW's net sales are direct Web sales.

Don't Abandon Print When You Go Online

When the World Wide Web first gained prominence in the mid-1990s, some pundits predicted the demise of most every other medium—particularly print. Yet successful online marketers have found that the strategic combination of print and online marketing methods optimizes their efforts. What's more, history shows us that new media do not obliterate old media, they simply sharpen the focus of each medium's function. As novelist and media philosopher Umberto Eco noted in the *World Press Review*, "The appearance of new means of information does not destroy earlier ones; it frees them from one kind of constraint or another." For example, television's swift rise to ubiquity with strong national networks and exceptional visual qualities did not "kill" radio in the 1950s. Rather, it inspired radio executives to reinvent their medium as a highly segmented, locally focused provider of music and information.

Jim Shanks doesn't believe CDW's use of multiple media will wane anytime soon. As he says, "CDW does tens of millions of catalogs a year, and every one of them talks about the Web. How many magazines would you have to take space ads in to get that kind of a circulation? Ed Bjorncrantz adds, "You have to send something out to the buyer to get them to come to the site. Should it be a brochure? A catalog? My suggestion is to test and make sure. A catalog designed for the Internet shopper that provides links to the product on the site would be a good thing. If you have an e-mail address, it's a very inexpensive way to advise customers that a catalog is coming, or tell them they just got a catalog and refer them to a promotion. You can also confirm their catalog orders via e-mail and reduce telemarketing expense in the process. Because of the J.C. Whitney brand and the 40 million catalogs we send per year, we can drive lots of people to the site that we would never have otherwise gotten. Or we can give people a more convenient way to reach us."

While Quixtar started as a pure-play Internet marketer without print support, its executives were quick to add catalogs to the mix. "We realized early on that we couldn't ignore print," says Ken Mc-Donald. John Parker adds, "Out of the gate, not having print support for Quixtar was a mistake, but we responded very quickly. If we had it to do over again, we would have had print right away."

Starting from Scratch Versus Retro-Fitting the Internet

Quixtar might have avoided its early "printless" problems if it had grown out of a seasoned direct marketing firm like J. C. Whitney or CDW, but it did benefit from being able to build its interactive database systems "from scratch." Although the firm did integrate information from the legacy system of its parent company Alticor, Quixtar has been treated as a start-up.

To avoid immediately confronting the problems inherent in this retrofitting process, some companies decided to set up their Internet businesses separate from the going business, often using outside vendors. J.C. Whitney was one of them, according to Ed Bjorncrantz. "J.C. Whitney started with a separate Internet group and now is trying to integrate with the rest of the organization. We knew going in it that doing the 'Net separately would be problematic down the road, but we also wanted to get up and running before the holiday season in 1997." By holiday season 2001, J. C. Whitney's customer service, database and catalog functions still were not totally integrated with its Web business.

Peapod, the Chicago-based online grocery business, had a similarly rocky period when it moved from a dial-up modem interface with proprietary software to an Internet ordering system. Thomas Parkinson of Peapod says, "The transition between the software and the Internet was difficult for us. In 1994, I launched a very sophisticated proprietary system and then a month later launched the Web site. Then I killed the proprietary system. Back then with the early browsers you couldn't do what you can today. It was painful for us, and for the customers." Peapod's Mike Brennan, adds, "When we went to the Web for the first time it was a step back for the consumer."

To their credit, both Omaha Steaks and American Blind and Wallpaper Factory have largely been able to avoid retrofitting problems due to excellent prior planning. Todd Simon of Omaha Steaks, recalls, "We integrated the 'Net fairly smoothly. We use the same order processing system as we do for phone or mail-in. The functionalities that pass information from the Web to the legacy system and back for tracking orders, sending e-mails, getting the right pricing and so on, are all centrally located. The main reason for our ease in transition is that we've done it all in-house. The same people who built our systems internally integrated the 'Net, so they knew what to do. To me, it's much more important to have your back end integrated than to have your channels integrated."

As Steve Katzman adds:

At American Blind we are control freaks. We do it all here, and we are team oriented. We were built for the Internet because we are really a virtual retailer. We have never maintained inventory, we don't have a warehouse or distribution, and all our product is drop-shipped from manufacturers. Here in-house we have the call center and the IT group. So we added on the new products that are Internet-only and built out the e-commerce channel, and already had the infrastructure to do it. We processed over 800,000 transactions during 2001. Many of the defunct pure-play Web businesses focused on the front end but got killed on the back-end. When we went online, we already had the infrastructure so that we could focus on the front-end experience for the customer.

Chapter Recap:

- The classic lessons of Integrated Marketing Communications (IMC) apply online.
- For strategic reasons, some firms may develop an online presence that does not fully integrate with its other marketing communications.
- Database integration across all media—including the Internet—is a must.
- Let customers buy when they want and through whatever medium they want.
- Don't abandon print communications when you go online.
- Some firms don't have this luxury, but building a system from scratch generally works more smoothly than "retrofitting for the Internet."

4 | New Savings— and New Costs

One of the most revolutionary aspects of Internet marketing is that it provides businesses with major opportunities to *save* money as well as *make* money. On the other hand, some of the overblown promises about "inexpensive Internet marketing" have gone completely unfulfilled.

The early days of the World Wide Web saw some naïve marketers envisioning a new medium that would cost them little or nothing to develop—and that would attract hoards of site visitors without much investment or effort on their part. Reality set in as firms found themselves budgeting six or seven figures developing an effective, fully functioning e-commerce presence to replace their original "brochureware." What's more, without skillful and sustained (read *costly*) site promotion, most companies attracted precious little traffic.

As the Web has matured, however, a number of bona fide money-saving opportunities have indeed presented themselves to marketers. Here are some of the best examples of "online economy"—as well as a few words of warning about potential Internet "money pits."

Bits Beat Atoms for Saving Money

As discussed elsewhere in this book, Web marketing does not eliminate the need for print promotion and/or support, but it may well lessen the necessary circulation and cost of these traditional media.

In his fine book, *Being Digital* (Vintage Books, 1996), Nicholas Negroponte talks about the differences between "atoms" that make up physical items such as direct mail packages, catalogs and magazines, and "bits"—the digital entities that make up an Internet image or message. Because direct marketers measure the ROI of every advertising method and medium, they've been quick to discover that the presentation of messages "in bits"—online and via e-mail—offers remarkable cost savings over "atomic" print media. A designer and writer still are needed to provide the pictures and words, and e-mail prospecting still may require expenditures for rented or purchased lists. Back-end functions must be developed and perfected as well. But the costs of print production, media and mailing are largely eliminated online.

What's more, many marketers have found that they now can use a simple postcard or self-mailer to alert customers and prospects to a robust new online catalog or other Web-based product offering. This is much less expensive than the full print catalog or elaborate direct mail package they might have used in the past.

Many a direct marketer has lamented the fact that his new catalog or her costly direct mail package became obsolete overnight because of price changes, product substitutions and the like. But online, fixes and updates can be made immediately and at very little cost compared to reprinting mailing pieces and catalogs.

Customers Actually Prefer Cost-Effective Methods

The expense of continued marketing to customers who buy online can be much lower than marketing to people who like to communicate about products via print and phone. Indeed, many online customers prefer to get their information strictly via e-mail and Web sites—and to purchase exclusively on the Web. Todd Simon of Omaha Steaks has found an additional benefit to this phenomenon. As he says, "The ongoing cost of marketing to Web-only customers is significantly lower, which means we can afford to market to them longer without dropping them."

In addition, because of the automation and self-service features on many sites, customer transactions online can be very cost-effective compared to print or other media. For example, the American Blind and Wallpaper Factory site is designed to make the search for wallpaper, blinds and other home decor items an enjoyable experience for the customer. This "sticky" site lets customers and prospects set up a Scrapbook of ideas for each room or area they are decorating and also send their selections to friends and family via e-mail for their input. If the customer wants the help of a human Personal Shopper, it is available, but many customers actually enjoy the anonymity and freedom of working out their own decorating schemes, according to American Blind's Steve Katzman.

With an average order including 35 items, Peapod has seen a definite savings when customers purchase autonomously online versus on the phone with a live customer service rep. As Mike Brennan explains, "A 35-item call is long and costly against profit. It is difficult to be 100 percent accurate when there is verbal order taking. There still may be a role for this option at a premium price."

A number of marketers find that product returns are lower among Internet customers, and they believe this may be because online customers can delve deeper to learn more about products before they buy. As Jim Shanks of CDW says, "People see their item pop up on the Web site and they know what they are getting. Online information does reduce customer service costs because it reduces returns. Self-service technical support on the Web saves money, too—although of course we are happy to provide live tech support for the customers who want it." Ken McDonald of Quixtar has also been pleased with his firm's low level of returns among online buyers. "Our primary brand names have a very low return rate of less than 0.5 percent," he reveals. "With a 100 percent money-back guarantee, that's pretty darn good."

Extranets Increase Information Flow— And Save Marketers Money

As the average cost of a personal sales call skyrockets to $300–500 and more, business-to-business marketers increasingly rely on database marketing and Customer Relationship Management initiatives to please customers cost-effectively. This appears to be a "win-win" initiative for many firms and their customers, according to Victor Hunter, author of *Business-to-Business Marketing: Creating a Community of Customers* (NTC/Contemporary, 1997). Ever since the early 1990s, Hunter's studies have shown the attentions of a face-to-face salesperson slipping substantially in customer rankings of importance.

Before the Internet, customers Hunter interviewed ranked the ability to get through to live, knowledgeable customer service phone reps as their number-one requirement. Now that many firms offer Extranets to their dealers and best customers, it is even more likely that costly face-to-face sales calls can be reserved for highly specialized services and breaking new ground rather than "maintenance." Extranets provide dealers and customers with vast amounts of customized data, even as they reduce the need for expensive personal sales interaction.

In addition to its customized Extranets, CDW has created CDWG, a separate Web site billed as "Your Technology Resource for Government and Education." Jim Shanks says that CDWG has provided a way to offer customized procurement systems for specific governmental agencies. Since these customized systems are automated, officials can purchase PCs even one or two at a time, cost-effectively on both sides.

Yamaha Band & Orchestral Division is developing an Extranet that will help its dealers break out of the "one big order" bind typical of past buying. As Gary Winder explains, "Our dealers traditionally have placed a monster order each year and often never change it." Glenda Plummer adds, "We pushed them to do that years ago for our own reasons—including keeping fulfillment costs down. Now that the dealers are becoming more business-savvy, they are rejecting that once-a-year concept and pulling product from us all year long. The Extranet will be helpful for this on both sides."

Winder envisions that before long, the Yamaha Extranet will provide value-added services to dealers and their employees with little incremental corporate cost. "Dealers will be able to assign different access levels to various employees. A salesperson in a store will be to look up product availability, buyers can place orders, and accountants can look up payment records—all by access codes."

Jeff Vredevoogd believes that Steelcase's e-Capabilities/Ensync is providing his firm with a major competitive edge within the office furniture industry. He notes, "Our focus is on the user, providing easy access to information—for our customers, for our dealers, for ourselves. Our solutions must enable the user to gain access to information that is important to them, when they need it. Individual access can be supported based on the customer's requirements. Ensync provides customers with flexibility to do what they want today, as well as evolve as necessary. In the end, time and money are saved all along the path. Customers can get what they need quickly without playing phone tag with their partners, dealers can provide additional service to the client, etc." Like Yamaha's new Extranet, Ensync allows employee-appropriate access to functions and data based on individual passwords.

Overturning Myths About Online Savings

While these online cost-saving stories are impressive, marketers also caution that not every promise of economical Internet marketing has panned out in practice. For instance, experienced marketers now say that in general, conversion rates are lower online than with other direct response media. American Blind's Steve Katzman laments the fact that his salespeople can't "grab hold" of a prospect online as they do in retail outlets or on the phone. "The 'Net puts the customer in total control of the process. You don't have the opportunity to ask for a sale or figure out their objection and overcome it. Our biggest disappointment with e-commerce is probably the lack of conversion. Even though we convert high relative to the industry standard on the Internet, it's 35 percent lower than what we do on the phone."

In addition, firms now realize that the cost of a Web site is not just its initial creation, but also its maintenance and upgrading on a sustained basis. At Quixtar, John Parker and Ken McDonald are working on finding effective ways to plan ahead yet still allocate resources to maximize emerging opportunities. "We're still looking out 12 to 18 months in terms of a planning business cycle and how to spend money," Parker says. McDonald notes that there are always more worthy online initiatives to pursue than the budget will allow. "No matter who you are you have limited resources or you will never make any money. You have to plan out quite a way to stagger the work load, but be flexible enough to change based on experience."

Perhaps most surprising is the fact that the much-anticipated savings on customer service have not panned out for many online marketers. Indeed, some firms have learned that Internet and e-mail customer service require different, higher-level skills and more time investment than traditional, phone-based service.

Steve Katzman says that customer service online "Does not reduce costs, it just shifts the cost. You can get things done much quicker with verbal communication on the phone and it's more efficient. The people you entrust to communicate via e-mail need a different and more extensive skill set than someone who is using the phone. E-mail customer service reps need spelling and grammar skills so your payroll costs are higher." Katzman's associate, Dan Gilmartin, adds, "You have to probe more with the written word to get to the heart of the problem." Thomas Parkinson of Peapod agrees, noting "E-mail results in multiple interactions rather than just one phone call."

To cut down on the need for written communicators, American Blind is migrating away from its online customer service chat function to "Live Help Now"—a call-back option. As Katzman explains, "'Live Help Now' works like a call center—it alerts the call center person to call a customer who has asked for help online. These phone conversations are much more efficient than the live chat. Average chat session takes 20 minutes while the average call-back takes 5. Asking for the order is easier on the phone than with chat, too. We do use scripts in instant chat because in 80 percent of the cases we know what the questions will be. Asking for the sale can be programmed in. In chat we have the reps ask a question with two positive answer options just like on the telephone. For example, 'Would you like to put that on your Discover Card, or 90 days same as cash?'"

John Parker of Quixtar comments, "The fallacy is that the Web creates lower costs for customer service. On a transactional basis it costs us a whole lot less to have an order come in electronically, but on the true customer service side, it's not necessarily less expensive and could be more expensive. Customer service functions are still more effective person to person over the phone. We do use some auto responses on e-mail. We have tried to determine that if someone asks this question, it's probably going to lead to these questions. So we build responses that answer all the upcoming questions. But I'm not sure automation is as effective in this area as a lot of people would make it out to be."

If everything goes well with a particular online order, however, there can be cost savings, according to Todd Simon of Omaha Steaks and Rich Burke of Spiegel. "The Web is a self-service environment," Simon says. "Self-service ordering and customers finding their own answer does help out on costs." Burke comments, "We have added a self-help feature to the Web site and about 40 percent of questions the customer can answer for herself.

It does lower customer service costs for us. Our cost to process a phone order is well over a dollar. For an Internet order it is pennies if the order fully integrates. Even considering the orders that 'kick out' we're talking dimes versus dollars."

Chapter Recap:

- Internet marketing offers potential savings, but not as universally as was originally predicted.
- Significant savings on print costs can be realized, using an economical mailing or ad to drive traffic to a robust Web site.
- Customers actually prefer some cost-effective Web methods such as:
  —Self-directed research, buying and customer service.
  —Robust Extranets.
- Online savings are not as extensive as once was hoped for reasons including:
  —Conversion rates are still relatively low.
  —Maintenance of Web sites can be costly and time-consuming.
  —Overall savings in customer service have not yet been realized in large part because e-mail communications are expensive.

5 | Speed-of-Light Testing

Testing has always been a way of life for direct marketers. Called "The R&D of direct marketing" by copy great Tom Brady, testing helps determine the most effective and efficient means of meeting business objectives, both offline and online. And now the Internet offers a huge advantage over all other media in that it allows for "testing at the speed of light."

Direct mailers may require weeks or even months to log test results that are conclusive enough for future planning. Magazines often have closing dates that are many weeks before the ads appear. and then responses may trickle in for months after the cover date. Because of their immediacy, newspaper and television ads offer quicker results once the ads are prepared and placed, but no medium compares to the swiftness of the 'Net. With skilled Webmasters on staff, marketing executives can establish testing parameters and go online in a matter of hours with various products, offers and creative approaches—then read the results in real time. They can eliminate poor-performing tests right away, or modify what's on the site if anything proves to be misleading or disadvantageous.

Marketers also are experimenting with segmented e-mail messages that click prospects through to specialized "landing pages" rather than the main Web site. There is a wealth of opportunity for e-mail testing here, too. For example:

- Sender names: What works best: an e-mail from the company CEO, a listing of the company name by itself, the name of a celebrity endorser, or other sender name?
- Subject lines: Does a price-related subject work better than a product-related subject? How about mention of time-limited special offers, savings, premiums, sweepstakes or contests?
- E-mail format: Does a simple, plain text message work better than an HTML image that may download slowly for some or be deleted by others for fear of an imbedded virus? What copy approach, length and tone work best?
- Multiple offers or one offer only: Should each e-mail focus on one simple concept and offer, or will you gain more total sales by making multiple offers with click-through options for multiple landing pages in one targeted e-mail?
- Landing pages: Once the e-mail recipient clicks through, what product(s) should be displayed and how many product(s) should there be? Will average order size improve if suggestions are made about accessories or add-ons to the main product shown?
- Transition to main Web site: Should visitors to the landing page be ushered quickly to the main site, or offered transport there only after they purchase something from the landing page?

When marketers first put up their Web sites and started using e-mail, most were focused solely on getting *something* online—there was little concern for optimization. And even today, few e-commerce companies are maximizing their opportunities to test products, creative presentations, layouts and the like. But there are some signs that smart marketers are beginning to apply tried-and-true testing methods to the online marketplace.

"Measure Everything"

Steve Katzman of American Blind and Wallpaper Factory takes a very analytical approach to his business. As he says, "We measure everything on sales per user session. We've been doing this for five years." However, he still finds controlled, direct mail-type testing problematic online. "In any type of program there are many variables, but in e-commerce there are 10 times the number of variables—so much on the site, so much that is dynamic in terms of functionality, connectivity and the like. It's difficult to isolate one change compared to a direct mail piece."

Dyed-in-the-wool marketers at Spiegel "test everything" online, according to Rich Burke. "It's the catalog mentality. We don't do anything without a test. We use control groups and standard testing methods online—the same things we have done for years offline. We don't test price but we do test promotions, layouts, heading changes and category changes. Every word on the site has been tested one way or the other. We don't test as much online as other media, but really it's just a little less."

Todd Simon says that Omaha Steaks is not yet doing as much testing online as he would like. "That's a function of our software. We need to re-architect the site to allow for testing, and once we do that we'll be doing a lot of testing. We're going to provide for A-B splits and other traditional testing methods. Eventually, we'd like to test online as much as in any other medium because we are 'testing freaks.' Soon, every Web promotion we do will have a test on it. So far we test offers and creative. We're also concerned about 'cart abandonment,' so we're observing and asking people why they don't complete the sale."

At Peapod, Mike Brennan also is impatient to find more and better ways to test. "We do classical direct marketing testing, but less online than in other media at this point. One thing we are testing is a control with no banner versus 1,000 people getting a banner ad with a special offer. Some people get a 30-cents-off banner, some get 50-cents-off, and some get a dollar off on Kraft cheese, as an example." The firm also does ongoing satisfaction surveys by e-mail to customers, and has response rates better than 40percent.

J.C. Whitney already has moved ahead into some more sophisticated testing methods, according to Ed Bjorncrantz. "The firm has the ability to deliver alternating presentations and track conversion, average order size, and so on. The alternates can be every-other visit, every-other hour, or another parameter." Bjorncrantz adds, "I don't think anybody does enough testing on the Web just like they don't in print media. The test logic has been better established on the mail side. Some of the things we'd like to track we can't at J.C. Whitney, but we can track how many times people are clicking certain features on the home page, and change the site accordingly to try to increase conversion and average order and opt-in and catalog requests."

Some Changes are Intuitive "Yes" Ideas

Even though many online marketers still don't have the sophisticated testing mechanism they'd like, many still believe they're making positive upgrades to their sites on a regular basis. As Steve Katzman says, "We get so much feedback from consumers and we don't leave a rock unturned. Being able to synthesize the information and making changes immediately—that's the power of the Internet. We have a survey on every product page, and we are looking for continual feedback. We get 500 to 600 survey responses each week. We don't hide from the customer, we rely on them. Most of the changes consumers suggest to us are so intuitive that we can just make them without extensive testing. There's so much low-hanging fruit that we don't have to worry about nuances at this point."

CDW has found real-time feedback very powerful as well. Jim Shanks recalls, "We had a new volume software license feature that was getting great activity but no sell-through. When the customer buys it, all they physically get is a piece of paper in the mail. When people got to the freight screen they were all bailing out. We realized—once customers complained—that we had a default in the system where if somebody didn't enter in a specific weight, our system entered 18 pounds times the number of licenses purchased. Some people wanted to buy 1,000 licenses at a time, so you can imagine what the freight charges looked like! Alarms started going off and we could fix it right away."

Rich Burke at Spiegel agrees with Katzman and Shanks. Online, he says, "There's not a lot of history. Some things you just have to do. Some changes are no-brainers."

Test Online—Then Move "Winners" to Print

Ed Bjorncrantz says that most online marketers should be able to test many new products online and migrate the successful ones to the catalog later on. Jim Shanks agrees, saying of CDW, "We'll run a pilot on things. By tracking our *Buyer's Edge* e-mail responses and the Buyer's Alert feature of our Extranets—which triggers an e-mail to the customer when a specified product hits a target price—we'll test a certain product on the Web and see if people are more interested in one price point or another. We use that knowledge for the printed catalog."

John Parker says that Quixtar has learned a great deal through a section of the Web site called Hot Buys: "This allows us to put special purchases on the site. They're not mainline products—could be anything from a Dodge Viper to watches, wearables and the like. As soon as they're gone we take them off the site. That generates excitement and re-visiting. But we can also take something off immediately if it doesn't sell. We can react quickly, take those lessons learned and address them in our other media."

Back Room Pre-Testing Helps Optimize Presentations

Because of all the things that can go wrong on a complex Web site or with a new system, form or layout, marketers are wise to do some serious pre-testing before launching features, designs and the like. At Yamaha, Gary Winder says, "We tested warranty registration for a couple of weeks within the company before putting in on-line. That way we could make sure it was easy for people to use, that all the fields were understandable and that information was going in the right places. When we're satisfied with something new, we send the piece to Yamaha corporate and they do their own testing before they upload it for us."

Randy Bancino says that Quixtar "has a whole team of people who constantly test in a quality assurance environment. When we first launched the site we tried to gauge capacity by having 100 computers 'pound orders' continually. Now our quality assurance is done with a version of the site that is only internal, and that only the cross-functional test team has access to. We'll try a test of 100 people putting in five orders and see what happens. Testing has changed a lot. In the old days you'd work on something for six months before launching it, but now we do a complete re-build of the site every two weeks. We have both a Webmaster and a Build-master—we call each new creation of the site a 'build.' Every two weeks there's a full redeployment of the site after the test phase. Every day, the content on the site changes with new text, pictures and promotions. We also do a lot of beta testing with our Independent Business Owners for major functions. We give our key customers access to test the new function and give feedback on whether it works for them."

Peapod also used a total of 500 beta testers before launching a new version of its entire Web site in October 2001.

When Action Performance joined forces with QVC, both companies worked extensively on design and testing. Steve Starkey from Action Performance's Information Technology department says of QVC, "They have teams that work on marketing and on the technical side. They also have a quality team from the business/operations side that checks on how orders work, how credit cards work, and so on."

Focus Groups Help Shape
Better Web Sites

Traditional focus groups are another pre-testing method that can be applied beautifully to the online environment. Indeed, for American Blind and Wallpaper Factory, talking to customers in focus groups led directly to the company's tagline, "Decorating so easy, it's fun!" Because focus groups showed the company how much customers hated the process of going to stores to buy decor products, they designed—and continue to enhance—their Web site so that it takes the drudgery out of shopping for wallpaper, blinds and wall art.

Peapod has both "guidance groups" and focus groups, according to Brennan. "Guidance groups are where customers come in and we talk to them about the site. The former director of research from Kraft does this for us." In addition to its own surveys and feedback from BizRate, CDW does "a traveling focus group where we go to several major cities once a year," Jim Shanks says. He continues, "We usually go to the top five cities (New York, Dallas, etc.) and we have customers come to CDW for technology seminars, at which time we ask several to participate in focus groups on subjects like Web site functionality."

Quixtar has done extensive focus groups as well as site usability tests. "One of the tests we had conducted on our behalf put people at screens on our Web site wearing special glasses that track their eye as it flows across the page. It indicates where they looked, and when," according to Ken McDonald. "It's 'space-agey cool'—but it also gives us a lot of new information to use in making our next set of decisions for the Quixtar site."

Chapter Recap:

- The Internet offers faster, more flexible testing opportunities than any other medium.
- E-mail testing also presents many valuable options.
- Test everything and measure everything to maximize online success.
- Some suggested changes are intuitive "yes" ideas that don't need extensive testing.
- Test online for fast answers and move "winners" to print.
- Back-room pretests and focus groups also help optimize online results.

6 | The Human Touch

In his mid-1990s novel *Microserfs* (HarperCollins, 1994), Douglas Coupland spun a "techy tale" through the narration of Dan, an ex-Microsoft programmer. As the book progresses, Dan embarks on both a garage-based start-up venture in Silicon Valley and a search for meaning in his personal life. Dan's geeky friends ponder whether they really need any "face time" with actual humans, meanwhile "coding" (computer programming) each day and night to the point of exhaustion. When engaged in a coding marathon, these digital warriors often eat only "flat food" (Pop Tarts, wrapped cheese slices and the like) pushed under the doors of their offices by concerned fellow workers.

While readers at first may despair for these obsessed and robot-like young people, Coupland ultimately offers a very positive message about the online world and its potential for facilitating human interaction. First, one of Dan's most introverted friends meets his soulmate through extensive online conversations. Knowing nothing about the other person's age, gender, nationality or color, Dan's friend declares his love for the chat pal based on intellectual and spiritual connection alone. At Coupland's rather Dickensian behest, the soulmate turns out to be an attractive, single female of similar age to Dan's friend. Then in a truly touching and more unexpected passage, Dan's mother—suddenly incapacitated by illness and unable to speak—finds a way to communicate digitally thanks to the efforts of Dan's own tech-savvy love interest (whom the mother had previously disdained).

Like Douglas Coupland, many philosophers and pundits have wrestled with the pros and cons of the Internet lifestyle. Naysayers argue that the Internet fosters isolation and anonymity. Marriages are broken and children are neglected by parents finding illicit romance in chat rooms. Teenagers are lured into face-to-face meetings with predators. Online gambling and pornography can lead lonely individuals into a destructive downward spiral. And even the community-building aspects of the Internet can be used negatively as individuals with antisocial or terrorist tendencies find kindred spirits online to encourage them and escalate their intentions.

While all of this may be true in certain cases, the Internet also offers an inexpensive, universal way for far-flung families and friends to engage in warm, cozy communication. The ever-growing number of family, wedding and new baby Web sites makes a positive argument for the Web's potential in connecting people. What's more, today's parents enjoy hearing much more regularly from their college-age and young adult offspring than they have in the past via Instant Messaging and e-mail. As one mother reports, "When I see both of my sons pop up on my AOL Buddy List each day, I know they're alive and well even if we don't talk. It's very comforting, and it keeps me from intruding too often on their busy lives with check-up phone calls."

Like all other communication media, the Internet indeed offers potential for both positive and negative interactions and outcomes. What's more, because of the absorbing, personal and interactive nature of the 'Net, these effects may well be magnified as compared to print, movies or television. As marketers explore this fledgling medium, they already have learned one very effective way to keep the 'Net's positive properties at the forefront. They strive to emphasize and optimize "the human touch" in their online and support efforts. Humanizing Internet marketing helps maximize opportunities for a civil, productive, positive and enduring relationship between companies and their customers.

According to Duncan Maclean, he and his fellow Mindpepper executives found personal, human contact the ideal antidote to online discourtesy. "People could sometimes be ridiculously rude in the e-mail feedback they sent us about bargainandhaggle.com," he says. "They thought they were talking to an unfeeling computer. When we politely contacted them—especially by phone—they immediately felt sorry and apologized, realizing that 'feeling human beings' have read their comments." Jennifer Jurgens adds, "Sometimes these customers would e-mail us back and apologize then."

Quixtar Puts Humans in the Online Mix

Quixtar executives attribute many of their firm's accomplishments to the combination of human interaction and online convenience. Quixtar's most successful offering to date—Ditto Delivery—works because an Independent Business Owner (IBO) takes his or her customers by the hand and leads them through this automatic replenishment plan. The process of setting up a Ditto Delivery account could be tedious if the customer had to do it alone—but with the experienced IBO guiding them through and asking all the right questions, customers cooperate readily.

As Quixtar's John Parker notes, "Two years ago Web people were laughing at us, saying the Internet was all about disintermediation, while we were setting up a site to work in tandem with personal interaction." His colleague Ken McDonald adds, "Think about it as a consumer. During the course of a week you might want a pair of pants, some vitamins and a good skin care product. Would you be more comfortable stumbling onto the Web and shopping around, or would you prefer to take a recommendation from a neighbor who is also an IBO?" Parker continues, "What may lead you to buy that specific skin care product for the first time is that your IBO neighbor loans you some. That leads to a conversation about other products." The IBO's personal recommendation is the key to success for Quixtar—indeed, individual customers cannot purchase from the Quixtar site without entering an IBO's number.

Avatars Humanize and Secure the Buying Process

Mindpepper's innovative one-to-one buying software has been a key to the astonishing growth of bargainandhaggle.com, but the addition of "warm-and-fuzzy" personal interactions has helped spur the site's expansion. Each transactor on bargainandhaggle.com is represented by an Avatar, described as "the online representation of a person's image in cyberspace that can be used to depict them as they move about the Internet." "Rookies" on bargainandhaggle.com are all assigned a Level 0 Avatar, the image of a newly hatched chick that Mindpepper executives call the "Funky Chicken."

As the site explains, "We assign every user a 'Rookie' or Level 0 Avatar right from the minute they sign up so that other users can easily recognize a brand new user. If you are an experienced BargainAndHaggle.com user, your Avatar will likely be a higher level. Please be nice to the Rookies and help them out whenever you can (they may not know their way around the site quite as well as you do), but be wary as they have probably not established a reputation yet either!"

Individuals who meet specific transaction goals move up to higher levels with corresponding perks and freebies from bargainandhaggle.com. What's more, since everyone is identified by level in the buy-sell arena, fellow transactors can find out who is seasoned and successful on the site. At higher levels, participants can select their own Avatars to help indicate personality style, gender and other attributes. What's more, buyers and sellers can read personal quotes from their fellow transactors, get level of service information, and see how many successful buying and selling transactions each participant has completed. There are even reviews from fellow transactors rating their buy-sell experience with each individual.

Personal Service Helps
Ensure Consumer Confidence

Thomas Parkinson of Peapod says that ordering groceries online is a terrific time-saver for consumers, but it is the delivery truck driver who makes buying from Peapod a "great experience." As he explains, "It's not about price—it's about not having to deal with this part of my life anymore." Peapod customers know their groceries will be delivered in a timely manner by a personable, courteous driver—what Parkinson calls a "consumer friendly driver." As Parkinson's colleague Mike Brennan adds, "The driver is the only person the customer sees. They can create a real bond with that driver."

Jim Shanks says that CDW has enjoyed cost savings through its Extranets and online technical information, but he cautions, "You can't eliminate your tech support people because you have the robust Extranet. If people want to do things electronically, great. But we have to have the human touch available if customers want it." That's why CDW assigns every buyer to a sales representative, even if the initial transaction is made 100 percent online. That rep receives commission on the sale and is available to the customer for future guidance and purchases.

Viral Marketing for Old-Fashioned Word of Mouth

While many failed dot.coms spent up to $2.5 million per 30-second spot on the 2000 Super Bowl, smart Internet marketers have found they can build awareness and referrals for next to nothing by implementing simple-yet-effective viral marketing programs.

Visitors to Omaha Steaks in the early summer of 2001 might have noticed a hot new Ford Thunderbird in the parking lot. The car was there as part of a joint-venture viral marketing event between Ford and Omaha Steaks. With a radio conglomerate in a nearby building, a remote broadcast was fairly easy to arrange while Omaha Steaks employees and folks from the surrounding industrial park gathered to feast on steak sandwiches and admire the new T-Bird model. Some marketers might write off such an event as "too local, too small in impact," yet when firms like Omaha Steaks take advantage of these opportunities wherever they present themselves, the long-term "word-of-mouth" effect can be powerful.

Peapod's Mike Brennan says he is "big into viral marketing as long as the program doesn't give me more people to manage. We create programs that have customers and employees sell memberships for us." On the back of Brennan's business card—and the business cards of everyone at Peapod—is a special, individual code. When a Peapod employee convinces a friend to sign up and buy online and enter the code, the employee gets $20.00. Customers can get similar referral fees when they invite friends to use Peapod. Brennan adds, "Now we're getting into school programs where we donate a certain percentage of sales to the school of the customer's choice. Our target customers are busy families with children." The school program can be promoted at the local level through simple flyers, meetings and affiliations with parent-teacher organizations.

In addition to its Live Help Now and Personal Shopper services, American Blind and Wallpaper Factory gains additional impact for its site with its interactive Scrapbook function. As the site explains, "Think of this as your home decorating scrapbook—a personal place that only you can access. Creating your scrapbook is fun, whether you're planning a real project or just dreaming about one. Use it to keep track of interesting products and ideas you find on our site and to compare samples. *You can even e-mail your scrapbook to family and friends to share your ideas and get their opinions.* It's easy to use, too. When you see something you want to remember, just click 'Save to Scrapbook.'"

Focus on Best Prospects for Effective Viral Marketing

Mindpepper has used a trial-and-error approach to viral and awareness-building marketing, with some notable failures that still have its executives chuckling and shaking their heads. As Duncan Maclean recalls, "To try to get new customers to register in late 2000, we developed a cartoon of a snowman who lost his nose, bent over and picked it up and blushed. We sent that to 250,000 people via e-mail and the vision was that at least 10,000 of those people would forward that on to 10 friends. New user registrations went through the roof for three hours and that was it. Catching people a few days before Christmas probably wasn't optimum, either.

"We also had this vision we would build momentum locally in West Michigan. We threw money at local media for a month and it was absolute flatline. The billboard company sent us a map that said 'here's where your billboards will be.' It looked good but we never seemed to drive past them. We did find them in some of the scariest neighborhoods in Grand Rapids—on the back of buildings with unlit billboards. We were buying smaller billboards—it was just a disaster. We were on local radio for months and got a total of maybe 60 users.

"One of the other failures from those days was thinking we could go door-to-door. We figured we could go to every little antique show in West Michigan, county fairs, antique malls and such, and get them to list things on bargainandhaggle.com. But these people didn't have computers except maybe a dusty old 286 in the back room, and they didn't have credit cards. One woman said the Internet was from the devil. We had a salesperson going door to door from January to April, 2001, and that resulted in all of one sale directly attributable."

Today in addition to their very successful e-mail solicitation efforts, Mindpepper has focused its viral marketing on a traditional direct marketer's "Invite a Friend" program offered online. As the site says, "Help us spread the word! If you have friends and family who would be interested in a smarter way to buy and sell online, let them know about bargainandhaggle.com. Just fill out the forms below and click on the Submit button. You can use our message or create your own." This way the firm encourages its own satisfied customers to identify their own "kindred spirits"—thereby building the base of individuals most likely to actively participate in bargainandhaggle.com.

Chapter Recap:

- While some pundits disparage the Internet as a cold and inhuman place, it actually offers great potential for unique human interaction.
- Smart companies find ways to "humanize" the online experience with person-to-person interaction, avatars or friendly home delivery.
- Viral marketing brings an old-fashioned method of personal communication to the online world.

7 | Exposing Sacred Cows: "Community" and "Stickiness"

"What we are really providing is a shopping tool for people, not a place to get together and whine," explains Catherine Ettinger, formerly of Mindpepper, when asked about community building on bargainandhaggle.com. Mike Brennan of Peapod adds, "We are a transaction site. Our customers don't want to chat and read. We help them shop fast and smart." His colleague Thomas Parkinson agrees. "If it doesn't sell something, why put it on? We are a home productivity package. Quicken manages your finances; Peapod manages your grocery shopping. Go to Ivillage.com if you want to chat. Come to us if you want to buy ketchup."

So much for the highly touted community-building aspects of the Web! Online experts charged with actually selling product on their Web sites consider community goals inconsistent with most e-commerce business models and not really necessary to success.

What's more, these e-commerce gurus are just as likely to throw cold water on the value of "stickiness"—at least in the aspect of getting customers and prospects to stay online for long periods of time. As John Parker of Quixtar notes, "We don't believe stickiness is a positive—we are going for quickness. Find the information, place the order, and move on. The model of getting and holding people is not necessarily what consumers want."

Early Internet marketing how-to articles stressed the essential nature of both community building and stickiness. But as it turns out, these values are mainly important for sites that need to keep Web surfers around to view advertising. Portals like Yahoo and CNN rightly believe that the longer visitors stay on their sites, the more likely they are to notice and click on advertising messages and offers. Thus they build content-heavy sites with "lures" to keep visitors online—and get them to return again and again. These include timely facts and news, regularly updated information, humor, puzzles, search functions, contests and the like.

The request of many such sites to "make us your home page" delivers the ultimate in both community and stickiness. In choosing that page to pop up every day, the viewer becomes at least a passive participant in its community. And what could be stickier than a page visitors see every time they boot up to their Internet browser?

When e-commerce marketers first started building their sites, many of them added features aimed at creating community and fostering stickiness. Some of them even harbored ambitions of becoming portal sites in their own right. But over the past few years most have become jaded about these so-called Internet "shoulds" of community and stickiness—and have either abandoned them or made sure they remain peripheral to the customer's ability to "get on, buy, and get off."

"Community" Opens
the Floodgates for Complaints

One of the highly touted aspects of the Web is its open availability to people all over the world, 24 hours a day, seven days a week. This can broaden a company's reach and potential for sales, but it also puts sites under a constant spotlight—and they're completely visible to critics as well as supporters. What's more, in the past naysayers might only tell their family and friends about something a company did that they didn't like, but on the Web a negative comment can be spread to huge numbers of customers, prospects and bystanders in a split second. Marketers know this is easy enough for negative people to do via e-mail and neutral bulletin boards. Many of them see no reason to create a forum for such commentary on their own sites.

As Joe Force, formerly of Mindpepper, says, "It's really only your angry customers who go to community areas on auction sites. It would be like McDonalds hosting a site where people could talk about what they found in their food or how dirty their bathrooms were. On the other hand, for bargainandhaggle.com, theoretically if we had collectors who were into art glass, they might build a community to talk about it positively. But they do that already on other sites or neutral forums like about.com." Ettinger notes, "there are quite a few other organizations that provide those forums, so we don't need to."

Duncan Maclean adds, "When you go to Auction Watch, you can see people saying almost literally, 'I am opening this thread because I had another bad experience.' There are some people whose glass is always half full, and others whose glass is always half empty." Force recalls, "One of the best examples was a message that said 'Bad check on bargainandhaggle.com.' Duncan ended up contacting the woman who posted that message, and he was told that she had already resolved the problem. The buyer made good on the check immediately for her, but the seller never went back online to say 'it's fixed.' We also don't want to have people in a community telling war stories about negotiating. We've seen people say things like, 'Wow, this guy is a really a sucker—I got this DVD player for $100!'"

While Yamaha executives see positives for community building among their dealers, they also see a possible downside. "Our Extranet has the potential to build dealer community," believes Gary Winder. "It will be a community in our eyes but we'll have to see whether the dealers view it that way. It depends whether they consider each other as peers or competitors. In a convention setting, they act like a peer group. In a business sense, sometimes they do not."

Supporting Communities
Not Worth the Expense and Effort

Steve Katzman of American Blind and Wallpaper Factory thinks "The whole community thing is overblown. What customers said originally is they wanted to be able to talk to people who had the same situation. We found that the instant chat with our customer service reps works for that. A lot of firms who didn't have that level of service with their own personnel used the bulletin board." But Yamaha has found that unless they monitor their bulletin boards and chat rooms, negative comments may be posted without rebuttal. While Yamaha realizes it would be unfair censorship to delete such comments, the firm does take the liberty of encouraging satisfied customers to counter the negatives with their own positive statements.

Action Performance used to support a close but expensive community via telephone but abandoned it when the firm went into partnership with QVC. Action Performance founder Fred Wagenhals considered the company's call center a central aspect of the collector's club that many customers enjoyed. QVC looked at the situation from a profit perspective—having reps chat about cars and races while selling only one or two model cars per call was cost-prohibitive. While Wagenhals laments the loss of that "club connection" and still fields customer complaints about it, Action Performance has no plans to re-implement the community online. "The QVC way makes money for the business," says Dave Martin of Action Performance.

Rich Burke at Spiegel also questions the value of an online community for his clientele. "With kids or seniors it might make sense, but for the average busy customer, no. You can stay online with our site and do a lot if you want, but we want to facilitate quick buying. Our peak time is 1 p.m. and again late at night—either at work on a lunch break or before bed. Our goal is to be as smooth and easy and nonobtrusive on the customer's life as we can. But at the same time, if she does want to see our virtual fashion shows, we'll have those available."

Omaha Steaks' Todd Simon adds, "We're not big on the community thing. We're pretty nuts and bolts about it: Do you want to buy the product or get information about it? We haven't seen that much need for chat about steaks and grilling."

John Parker of Quixtar says that the company's Independent Business Owners fulfill customers' need for community. "The meetings and interactions IBOs have with customers are important. Also, the IBOs work together to learn, succeed and grow their businesses. We've been successful building community with an Internet business, but the community is not online."

In its early days, Quixtar tried to be a portal and featured some involvement devices that it abandoned fairly quickly. Randy Bancino says, "On the same day we dreamed up Ditto Delivery (the firm's successful ship-'til-forbid program), we also thought up something called MyQuixtar—a personalized portal with news feeds and the like. It never took off because people prefer the Yahoos and AOLs of the world. We weren't adding any significant value in that space. We also tried offering a series of interactive online faces so customers could find one similar to theirs and 'put on make-up.' And we let people build a table setting online with dinnerware patterns they liked. Things that are 'just plain cute' like that get a big spike and then usage just plummets. These features attracted some excitement, but they're not long-term components of our site."

Sites Will Offer "Sticky Aspects" for Those Who Want Them

While most executives do everything they can to avoid putting roadblocks between online customers and a sale, some do see the value in strategically and carefully adding "extras" for those who enjoy them.

For example, while Kevin Giglinto of the Chicago Symphony Orchestra says, "My number-one priority is ticket functionality," he is thinking of adding a subscriber forum to the CSO site. "Along with this would come the ability to log in and see your account, and get a receipt for your donation. But even just putting a forum online means you have to monitor it and see what's put up there. Staffing-wise and budget-wise, we are pretty tight."

At Spiegel, Rich Burke says that every piece of additional content for the Spiegel site will be tested to make sure it's a plus before it is added permanently. "We'd like to add some reasons to come back to the site other than shopping so people will be curious what's new there," he says. Spiegel's success offering horoscopes has spurred Burke on to test the addition of information on "women's health, family issues, styling tips for the home and for her. If it works we will roll it out, if it doesn't we'll stick to e-commerce." Products offered on horoscope pages have had impressive sell-through rates, so Burke will be looking for similar quantifiable evidence that specific content leads to incremental sales.

Thomas Parkinson of Peapod has learned from watching the successes and failures of the financial site Quicken, which he sees as a similar "home productivity package" to Peapod.

> At Quicken they kept listening to their top 5 percent 'power users,' and their product became too complicated. We don't want to 'Quickenize' our product. In the long run, building community is important and it's in our plans. We already have a feature that lets people sort in a category by what products are most popular. I can see letting people click and talk, having reviews of products including what others have said about this product. We want to do what's convenient, not what's unbelievably sophisticated.

Chapter Recap:

- Community may be an overrated online virtue because:
  —Getting people to shop is much more important.
  —Communities may breed complaints and negativity.
  —They're not worth the effort and expense they require relative to their results.
  —Only a small percentage of visitors really crave community on most sites.

- Stickiness may be an overrated online virtue because:
  —Quickness and functionality are more important to most visitors.
  —Features developed to improve stickiness often spike up length of visit in the short term, but soon are virtually ignored.

8 | Mars and Venus Come to Terms

When John Gray—author of the highly successful *Men Are from Mars, Women Are from Venus* books—finally loses his luster on the seminar and TV talk show circuit, he might just pursue a new niche for his work. Gray would find plenty of "relationship issues" to explore in the marriage of marketing and information technology. Long a source of aggravation for both sides, their communication problems and at-odds goals have usually been ignored or skirted. Indeed, some vendors have made a fortune developing separate "desktop databases" that let decision makers steer clear of the IT mainframe, yet still gain retail and direct marketing intelligence.

Work-arounds and avoidance tactics may allow staffers to muddle through in a bricks-and-mortar or traditional direct marketing environment, but when a company goes online, it becomes essential that IT and marketing work harmoniously together. As e-commerce experts Bernice Grossman and Ruth Stevens suggested in a recent talk at a Direct Marketing Association convention, the process requires executives to:

- Look for antiquated, redundant or unwieldy processes in the firm's traditional direct marketing methodology.
- Automate what works well.
- Reengineer or eliminate the bad.

To achieve this, Grossman and Stevens counsel firms to:

- Develop a team of IT and marketing people.
- Isolate them—a country retreat is good.
- Encourage them to find new ways to work together for online success.
- Work out technical problems before the launch.

As Grossman and Stevens point out, valued customers who go online to a trusted source are expecting the experience to be seamless. Yet in the online environment, there is little opportunity for human intervention to smooth over problems and offer alternate solutions. Thus if any disfunction between IT and marketing shows up in online hiccups, the firm in question stands to lose good customers online—even those who have been well satisfied buying through other media and channels.

Working Out the Glitches Takes Time and Effort

While most marketing executives agree with the suggestions of Grossman and Stevens, some have found the integration of IT and marketing a definite challenge. As Glenda Plummer of Yamaha reports, "It has been a real battle. The IT person thinks he's in control, creating a struggle between marketing and IT. Lately, the power for the Web site has been moved from IT into marketing." Yamaha's Gary Winder adds, "The look of the Web site under the IT guy's direction was very stale. Our VP and General Manager understood that marketing had to hire its own Web person. This new Web manager is proactive whereas under IT it was reactive. He's passionate about updating and improving our information regularly."

Rich Burke of Spiegel agrees that support from the top is essential in making sure marketing's online IT needs are met. "You can't do much (online) without IT assistance, but our management is behind it."

At Steelcase, Jeff Vredevoogd notes, "We are fortunate to have a strong team of IT professionals who are intelligent, experienced and creative. Bringing a marketing guy like me into an IT-related organization has not been without its challenges. In the past, we may have looked at things and approached things differently. Today, we operate as a single team—Marketing and IT work side-by-side reviewing customer needs, formulating solutions, and so on. The more we can bring the needs of the user to the table, the better we all are in providing solutions that exceed the needs of our customers. We rely and depend on each other."

Marketers Must Learn to Speak IT's Language

While some firms have made progress with management-led initiatives to put marketing in the driver's seat for online development, experts agree it's still essential that online marketers learn more about IT than their offline counterparts.

As Ed Bjorncrantz says regarding J.C. Whitney, "With catalogs, the marketer's primary involvement was merchandising and creative.

Those are still important but it has to get implemented from a technology standpoint. For most marketers, the challenging part is that you have to understand technology and understand the investment in technology since the Internet has a lot more technology issues than do catalogs. We clearly now have an additional partner in IT that we never had before in marketing. We're now faced with integrating merchandising, development and creative for both offline and online media. The Internet will be the conduit for product introduction and you can't have two merchandise flows. I believe you have to have the development in IT if you plan to be Web-based going forward. You need to re-develop the existing system with the Internet in mind."

Thomas Parkinson of Peapod believes, "Most marketers aren't trained in personalization. Somebody has to manage the rules of personalization. Getting down to one-to-one is really a self-running system that requires management of the business rules. You need people who can understand it and manage it—when to shut something off and when to implement it. It's a challenge to find marketing people who also want to develop and manage tedious business rules."

Jennifer Jurgens, formerly of Mindpepper, adds, "Where technology and marketing overlap in our company is in product development. Getting those visions all synched up is challenging. The basic problem is to get people coordinated and on the same path at the same time. It was important that we included Joe Force, our Chief Technology Officer, in this dynamic. There was a good amount of mocking and teasing back and forth in a fun, Dilbert sort of way. It's important that the marketing person understands some of the technology but freely defers to the IT people. It's also vital to have an IT person who cares enough to listen to 'marketing needs this because.' Open communication is the key."

Joe Force comments, "I thought it was going to be a bigger issue, but I believe that Jenni and I were able to work well together.

I don't know if that would be the case with a traditional marketing person who didn't know anything about technology."

The Ideal IT Person for E-Commerce Is a "Closet Marketer"

Steve Katzman of American Blind and Wallpaper Factory says that internal controls and a cross-functional team approach help keep IT and marketing focused on the same page. Even so, he admits, "We are pretty fortunate to have a couple of IT guys who are frustrated marketers, so they really love this challenge." In addition, Katzman finds it helps to "keep the company consumer focused rather than allowing internal power struggles to develop."

At Omaha Steaks, Todd Simon uses similar strategy. "Marketing and our customers lead the charge. We react to how customers are reacting to our business. IT has given marketing the tools to merchandise the site, and IT gets more involved in functionality issues, complex testing and the like. I do joke with our CIO that we are going to turn him into a marketing manager yet!"

Internal Controls Keep the Process Running Smoothly

Parkinson and his Peapod colleague Mike Brennan believe that their internal systems help keep IT and marketing working well together. Parkinson observes, "We've done a pretty good job of developing very flexible rules-based systems that let marketing do promotions on the Internet. We have a workflow system in Lotus Notes where marketing enters a work request that goes to the content department, which interfaces with IT. We've built the system such that the content people can really implement on their own. Brennan concedes, "Marketing has to understand what's possible to deliver to customer segments, and develop customer focused business rules within those parameters."

Katzman has found that using outside vendors can impede the IT/marketing process. "The problem with all these third-party operations is that we are pretty sophisticated and we know what we want to do and how. Vendors will say "We can do it, we can do it," but when you ask them to put it in writing they say they're not quite so sure." That's why American Blind tends to build new processes with its internal cross-functional teams even if it takes longer. "We live and die by technology and functionality," Katzman says. We have historically found it's less expensive to build and maintain our own; and the flexibility to change it as needed."

Homegrown Talent vs. Dot.com "Stars"

Because many of the integrated "clicks-and-mortar" companies are in exotic locales like Omaha, Nebraska or Grand Rapids, Michigan, visitors won't find too many ex-Silicon Valley "stars" on their IT and marketing staffs. Indeed, many firms prefer to use local talent or grow their Internet staffers from within. Those who do want staffers with dot.com experience find them much easier to acquire in recent months. "It's changed a great deal since the dot.com crash," says Burke of Spiegel. "A couple of years ago we couldn't hire quality people; they wanted out-of-this-world money. Now you can get quality people at affordable prices."

American Blind and Wallpaper Factory of Plymouth, Michigan, does not import people from Silicon Valley, according to Katzman. "Most of our people are home-grown," he says. "They grew up in our IT department. Many are legacy IT people who learned and adapted to the new technology, then we added some new hires from outside the company with ASP-focused background. We don't have to extend the search beyond the Detroit area." Dan Gilmartin says that American Blind doesn't have much turnover. "We haven't had any relocations of IT staff, not even in the top job."

"Yamaha has a tradition of allowing people to become specialists in the area for which they have a passion," according to Glenda Plummer. "This fosters dedication and longevity in our employees. We also allow people to try new things if we believe a job opening may be a fit for them. Yamaha believes we can teach smart people the skills necessary for a new position if the basic qualities and most important, the desire is there."

Chapter Recap:

- Before the Internet, IT and marketing personnel often could work around each other and avoid confronting their differences. That's no longer the case.
- Operational glitches in traditional selling methods must be identified and overcome so customers can function independently and happily online.
- Marketers must learn to speak IT's language to work online.
- Good online IT people often are "closet marketers."
- Internal controls and clear expectations help bring IT and marketing together.
- Growing e-commerce personnel internally may help avoid IT/marketing culture conflicts.

9 The Challenges Ahead: Four Areas of Focus

Imagine paying $2,250 plus a horse and carriage for a single tulip flower bulb. That would be shocking enough today, but in 1624 a white and maroon 'Semper Augustus'-type bulb commanded that price—unadjusted for inflation—fueling the so-called "Tulipomania" in The Netherlands. The story continues on www.bulb.com: "In 1637 the tulip trading crashed. People who thought of themselves as extremely rich were reduced to poverty overnight. In spite of the uproar and the difficulties that accompanied the wild speculation in tulips, the tulip continued to be the most popular garden flower for a very long time. . . . The lasting Dutch fascination with tulips—and enduring Dutch flower industry—owes at least part of its development to Tulipomania."

It took more than a decade for the Dutch tulip market to evolve from its heights to the depths of despair, while the peak of dot.com fever lasted only a couple of years. Perhaps we can attribute this disparity to the concept of "Internet time"—the equivalent of "dog years"—in which the Internet business moves seven times faster than the actual passage of weeks and months on the calendar.

While pundits and journalists try to convince readers that dot.coms are "over," students of economics know that the shakeout of 2000–2001 represented a natural and necessary life cycle stage for any product or marketing channel. Even so, it may be too soon for the many former "stock option paper millionaires"—still licking their wounds and looking for well-paying jobs—to acknowledge that the dot.com crash was a blessing in disguise. As Randy Bancino of Quixtar explains it, "We're in that unfortunate but predictable part of the curve. The whole Internet industry got overhyped, and now we are in the backlash period where every idea from that era must have been a dumb idea."

On the other hand, most of the executives interviewed for this book have cut their losses, learned from their mistakes, and rolled up their sleeves for the real work of building a sustainable online business. They point to several areas of specific focus that will help them improve their profit margins, forge deeper and more lasting relationships with customers, and broaden their market potential. Many of them also have words of wisdom to share about how Internet businesses can position themselves for maximum success in the long run.

Focus Area #1: Overcoming Cart Abandonment

While many traditional direct marketers have been able to run profitable businesses with extremely low response rates, they have always been disturbed by their inability to convert sales at higher levels. This frustration is difficult enough to bear without proof that a customer actually looked at your offer and then rejected it for some reason. But now on a Web site with a well-designed back end, a marketer can trace its customers' and prospects' every move . . . right up to the time they either buy or "walk away."

As Todd Simon of Omaha Steaks says, "The data from one user session is immense. We have developed a method to look at that interactively. Any of our managers can go in and look at the statistics of what's going on, but what we can do with that information has yet to be defined." Simon plans many more tests of offer, creative, and getting the best possible traffic to the site. As he explains, "We work with partners to try to drive more traffic among people who have an affinity toward our product or are 'transactors'. They want to buy via the Web. The abandonment issue is big here—we see cart abandonment of 50 to 60 percent. We have an internal group looking at customer comments, usage statistics and the like to see if clusters of consumers are abandoning at certain points. We will continue observing and asking people in order to determine what improvements we can make."

At Peapod, according to Mike Brennan, "Only 12 percent of the people who come to our Web site and enter a viable zip code finish an order. We would like to make that number higher and higher. Of the people who do place an order, we need to improve the percentage of those who come back—who move from trial to ongoing usage. If we can get them to order a third time, they're hooked."

Kevin Giglinto of the Chicago Symphony Orchestra realizes, "If you have people creating carts and not buying, they might just be people who don't like to buy online. We get students who do a lot of shopping but no buying." But on the other hand, he has observed that in the past, the symphony lost customers if they asked for specific seats but couldn't get them. "You can see if they get delivered their ticket offer online and they say, 'uh . . . no.' The way

I'm trying to change that is to have the whole available inventory online rather than just a block of tickets. Also, I have asked our IT department to find me some better tracking software so I can find the most frequent drop-off point. Then I can see what specific pages may be creating problems."

Focus Area #2: Streamlining and Search

According to a study by the Direct Marketing Association released in January 2002, online marketers now are focusing attention on making Web sites easier for consumers to use. This includes "reducing the number of clicks to checkout and offering real-time inventory information and search features." For example, according to this study, conducted for the DMA by The E-tailing Group Inc., in late 2000 the average number of clicks required to buy an item was 8.76. By the end of 2001, it was down to 5.36 clicks.

Other areas of Web site improvement include provision of real-time inventory status, improvement of search features, availability of privacy policies, provision of e-mail confirmations for shipment, and special toll-free telephone numbers for online customer service. To conduct the study, researchers bought one product from each of 100 commercial Web sites during fourth-quarter 2001. Items were grouped into 16 categories, including apparel, books and music, computers, consumer electronics, department stores, gifts and home and garden.

Because of the great potential for easy-to-navigate Web sites that are deep, wide and cost-effective to create, experts agree that an e-commerce venture offers opportunities for much more than a simple "catalog online." As marketers hone and perfect their Web sites, many plan to find better methods of "slicing and dicing" their offerings online—and to improve their search functions.

As CDW's Jim Shanks says, "On the Web site you can't 'scroll and page' like people are willing to do in a catalog. You have to be more concise. To me, you see the scrolling and paging down and the long copy coming from people with traditional marketing backgrounds rather than IT and Internet backgrounds. We don't want anything flashy—that's not what our customers want to see. Our goal is to help them find things quickly as possible, tell them everything they want to know, help them purchase efficiently, and then deal with post-sale issues." Thomas Parkinson agrees, saying that at Peapod, he's willing to set up the site to "sort by unit price, fat content, whatever is important to the customer."

With hundreds of thousands of SKUs available through its own product offerings and those of partners, J.C. Whitney must develop ways to help customers find what they want as quickly and painlessly as possible—while still creating opportunities for up-selling, cross-selling, and impulse buys. As Ed Bjorncrantz maintains, "J.C. Whitney is not an impulse buy company. Customers are looking for a specific product for a specific application. This is more search oriented, with people searching by product category, by make and model, or by term. You need to spend considerable money improving your search, and there's always more you can do to enhance it. You also want to limit the number of steps to buy."

Jeff Vredevoogd, of Steelcase Inc., faces a more complex challenge. "Steelcase's future is providing a complete, comprehensive, integrated solution that supports the customer's entire facility management process. Our focus is more than simply to streamline the procurement of a new chair. Customers expect more. This requires customer-driven solutions that integrate with both Steelcase and its dealers."

Focus Area #3: Selecting and Measuring Banner Ads and E-Mail Lists

When the first banner ad appeared on *Wired* magazine's HotWired.com in October 1994, the advertising world took notice. This was a whole new targeted medium combining elements of the general advertising billboard as well as direct marketing and sales promotion. For a time in the mid-1990s, advertisers willingly signed contracts to pay for banners on a CPM rate based on "impressions, not actions." And as recently as 1999, some sites could convincingly promise average click-through rates in the 2 percent range. But with the proliferation of Web sites and banner ads, click-through rates plummeted. And with direct marketing-types demanding quantifiable results from their banner ads, the fledgling medium entered a period of turmoil.

While companies like Mindpepper and American Blind and Wallpaper Factory have been driving increasingly hard bargains in the early 2000s to bring new prospects and customers online, other firms have soured on banner advertising for prospecting. "Banners didn't work," says succinct Action Performance accounting-type Dave Martin. Jim Shanks of CDW adds, "There were companies with a year or two years of extensive marketing budgets dedicated to banners that yielded zero." Steve Katzman of American Blind will do "very focused banner ads that are tied specifically to key word searches like wallpaper and blinds. We buy them on a CPC (Cost Per Click) basis; very little on CPM unless it's under $20 a thousand." Todd Simon will pay even less than Katzman on a CPM basis for Omaha Steaks. As he says, "We only do banner ads on a per-click or per-order basis. We ran run-of-site ads on a CPM basis at $5 a thousand because targeting didn't pay out at $40 a thousand."

Frustrated by low click-through rates and elusive measurement methods, these firms clearly aren't receiving the conversion rates they originally expect from online advertising, nor are they convinced of its brand-building potential. On one point most experts do seem to agree: The days of paying for banners and e-mail prospecting on the basis of healthy CPM rates are long gone.

While ad serving companies and agencies seek more attention for banners of different shapes and sizes that appear over, under and throughout Web sites with motion, sound and other attention-getting aspects, client companies seek more accountability for the ads that they place. One possible positive move is the introduction of online advertising guidelines from the trade group Interactive Advertising Bureau.

Developed after a six-month study by PricewaterhouseCoopers, the guidelines attempt to define five key metrics for online advertising: impressions, clicks, visits, unique visitors, and page impressions. They are available at www.IAB.net. It remains to be seen whether the industry will adopt them, but the IAB claims its members represent more than 70 percent of the advertising sold online.

Focus Area #4: Strategic Decisions About International E-Commerce

For many Internet marketers, finding a way to succeed domestically has been challenging enough over the past few years without layering on international concerns. But considering the potential for growth in Europe, Asia, Latin America and other parts of the world, a more global vision seems warranted for many firms in the near future. And because Web sites are visible anywhere in the world, it's almost inevitable that most firms will receive some inquiries from outside the U.S.

The Chicago Symphony Orchestra sees orders coming over the transom from Western European countries and Japan, where the orchestra plays fairly frequently. While Kevin Giglinto does not actively solicit such orders yet, he fulfills them "If DHL goes there," as he reports. Dan Gilmartin says that American Blind has a similar philosophy, except that their international "shipper of choice" is UPS. Ed Bjorncrantz says that while J.C. Whitney does sell internationally, the company's approach is "not optimized."

Omaha Steaks also takes a low-key approach. As Todd Simon comments, "The logistics of shipping our product over borders is so difficult that we do it only on a case-by-case basis. It hasn't been a significant vehicle for us. Were we to do this and if there weren't those shipping barriers, I would see it as a very important tool. I can see how international sales are important in general." Peapod's parent company owns the largest grocer in the Netherlands, and the various organizations trade knowledge about online sales back and forth, according to Thomas Parkinson.

On the other hand, Mindpepper was given a mandate to move forward on international operations for bargainandhaggle.com in mid-2001. "The BDO Seidman board (parent of Mindpepper) said 'go international and go now,'" reports Duncan Maclean. Jennifer Jurgens adds, "Our chairman of BDO believes in international. It comes from the top with full support." Thus the site was to move beyond its current focus on the United States and Canada. The process may be quite involved, Maclean believes, "Because our terms of service need to be legal, and it's a lot of expense to determine that in other countries. We also want to ensure our sellers that they won't get embroiled in international transactions."

Mindpepper considered various alternatives including encapsulating all selling by country or opening up buying and selling internationally and letting customers determine whether they want to participant beyond their own borders. "We could make it all English and allow transactions only in U.S. dollars," Maclean adds. "We could also look into partnering, licensing or strategic alliances.

The vision technically was that it would all be one database." Beyond the technical concerns, Maclean and Jurgens were focused on making sure they were sensitive to all cultures. "The concept of 'haggling' is very different in various cultures," Jurgens notes.

BDO Seidman's focus on an international presence for bargainandhaggle.com is borne out in a recent report by research firm Jupiter MMXI. It shows that European online sales for the holiday season 2001 were estimated at 2.9 billion Euros (approximately $2.59 U.S. dollars at that time). That represents an increase of 71 percent over the year 2000, in a time period where recessionary woes kept U.S. holiday sales at much tamer levels. As Jupiter analyst Patricia Laueer noted, online retailers experienced a real growth in the usage of the sites in the run-up to Christmas, which shows just how Europeans have come to accept the Internet as part of their lives." Booksellers including Amazon and W. H. Smith dominated the sales picture in much of Europe, while venerable British retailer Marks and Spencer also made a splash in the U.K.

Going Forward: Words to the Wise

With a decade or less of online experience to draw upon—and a market that often changes direction without warning, rhyme or reason—it may be unfair to ask Internet executives for future prognostications. Even so, many answer without hesitation when asked for wisdom to share with fellow online marketers.

For example, Todd Simon of Omaha Steaks takes a strict dollars-and-cents approach. "You have to make a smart marketing investment—know how you're driving traffic and have very clear understanding of your own customer lifetime value model. This lets you understand how much you can spend to acquire a customer. You can't have a sustainable business unless you spend less to acquire customers than their long-term value." Mike Brennan of Peapod calls this "business physics." He adds, "There are certain forces of why a business works. How people shop, what's feasible, selling to them at a distance. Where people say 'this old way doesn't apply,' we have to find a new way to bridge the gap between the past and the present."

Dave Martin of Action Performance counsels that selling on price is a dead-end proposition. " It seems to me the whole issue of online success is related to technical capability—both in merchandising and IT—and the ability to attract people to your Web site who are coming there for reasons other than bargains."

Steve Katzman of American Blind emphasizes the importance of strong operational underpinnings. "Almost anybody can create a Web site today and even an e-commerce site, but it's a whole other thing to have the back end. People put the cart before the horse when they focus on the front end. You spend so much money getting the customer to come to your site that to screw it up because you don't have the infrastructure is a self-defeating process." Randy Bancino of Quixtar expresses similar sentiments. "When developing customer relationships you should build your business from the back to the front. You should over-deliver on customer expectations. The site needs to load fast and be easy to navigate. Customers will forgive you if you don't have bells and whistles but will not forgive slow loading sites and packages that don't show up. At Quixtar, we have stuck to blocking and tackling."

Katzman also notes that online customers are a different breed from those that many established businesses are used to serving in a storefront or telemarketing environment. "While the consumer who is buying online may look demographically like your traditional consumer who shops at brick and mortar or on the phone, you are missing the boat if you leave it at that. The person who shops online might never go into your store—they have a different psyche than the retail shopper. The real challenge is to expand your market share by providing a new way to buy for this different consumer."

Diana Rodriguez-Velazquez of Carnival Cruise Lines believes that many Web sites have a long way to go in terms of building and supporting the brands they represent. "You must deliver the brand with every click," she comments. Bancino adds, "You can't overcome brand—you either have it or you don't and if you don't you're in a bad place."

Take Some Risks in This New Medium

While Jim Shanks echoes the bottom-line approach of Simon and Brennan, he also believes that this largely uncharted territory allows for some stretches marketers might not make in more traditional media. "My advice is to determine what you want to be, create a business model that supports it, and stick to it! Measure everything, but don't overanalyze or get preoccupied with the data. It's such a quick feedback loop that there's no reason not to try a campaign or an idea. It's an incredible environment for risk-taking. You can tell very quickly if people like something or not."

Duncan Maclean, formerly of Mindpepper, reminds Internet marketers, "Nobody has done this before. No matter how much we read and talk to people, there is no right answer and no definitive approach. It's one thing to react quickly and another to have instant access to data, but it's still another to really know if you are right or wrong. If something's working, you're an expert. Two weeks later, if it's not working, you're an idiot!"

Maclean's former colleague Joe Force concludes, "The Internet is changing very quickly, and what we were doing six months ago we thought was absolutely right. It even may have been right then but now it isn't, and we have to change. What we now think is the absolute center of bargainandhaggle.com may only be a small piece of it in a year. Anything from a typo to a whole program can be tweaked or fixed with this medium. We may not do it right the first time, but we have to do it and do it until we get it right!"

Chapter Recap:

- Areas of focus moving forward for online marketers include:
  —Overcoming cart abandonment.
  —Streamlining and search.
  —Selecting and measuring banner ads and E-mail lists.
  —Strategic decisions about international e-commerce.
- Words to the wise: focus on measurement, branding and the back end—and be willing to take some risks.

II | *The Leaders*

10 Action Performance: Synergy with Partners
www.qvc.com/goracing.html
www.action-performance.com/

Most financial analysts thought NASCAR collectibles marketer Action Performance (ACTN, Nasdaq) was headed for a smash-up during the fourth quarter of 2000. The stock hit a low of 2-⅜ (off from $48 just months before), making the rest of the dot.bomb-plagued Nasdaq look flush by comparison.

Action Performance enjoyed a rabid fan base among enthusiasts of NASCAR and other high-performance auto sports, and its collectibles continued to command impressive prices on both the primary and secondary markets. But the firm had sunk considerable money and toil into the Internet with poor results. And that effort—combined with other market forces—had placed Action Performance's future in jeopardy.

While many Nasdaq high-flyers crashed and burned, Action Performance CEO Fred Wagenhals absolutely refused to admit defeat.

A flamboyant and colorful character, Wagenhals collects full-size classic cars and other pricey "toys" to show off in his personal museum at Action Performance's Phoenix headquarters. A renowned risk-taker, Wagenhals mortgaged his Scottsdale home a decade ago to provide a $300,000 advance on royalties to the late NASCAR legend Dale Earnhardt. Even today, Earnhardt collectibles bring Action Performance tens of millions of dollars in annual revenues, and the firm boasts exclusive relationships with other top drivers like Jeff Gordon, Bobby Labonte, Dale Jarrett and Dale Earnhardt Jr.

Through contacts in the Phoenix financial community, Wagenhals handpicked Dave Martin to lead a dramatic financial turnaround for Action Performance. Martin was a successful CPA who had tried early retirement, but could not resist the challenge Wagenhals presented. In September 2000, Martin moved back to Phoenix from his California vacation home and rolled up his sleeves as Chief Financial Officer for Action Performance. Wagenhals turned over the company's financial reins to the low-key Martin. His charges to the new CFO were to stabilize and rebuild the company's financial position—and to help find a way for the firm to thrive both online and offline.

The results of Martin and Wagenhals' combined efforts have made Action Performance one of the few firms to hit the dot.com skids and then rebound. Indeed, with ACTN up 1200 percent during the first 11 months of 2001, *The Arizona Republic* declared Action Performance "Arizona's Hottest Stock."

A Pragmatic New Plan for the Firm's Web Presence

As part of his immediate triage plan, Martin temporarily shut down Action Performance's online consumer marketing. "What we did as of September 2000 was nothing direct-to-consumer," he recalls. "Our goracing.com site started as a portal, and it failed like all others of that ilk. It had advertising and content. The idea was for people to come for that on a regular basis and then stay to buy product. That didn't work for anybody! Go Racing was an established brand before the site went online, and Action Performance thought that racing fans would be drawn there, but that didn't happen. When I came into the company nobody wanted to talk about goracing.com."

Martin says that financial analysts and others "hoisted" goracing.com's failure as the reason the company had fallen on hard times. While it was really only a contributor to the problem, he notes, "The company did not have a lot of capital resources at the time and the last thing we were going to do was bring up any kind of Internet site that would require an investment. Even if you sold a large amount of product, Internet sites were not profitable; for a little company like ours (2001 sales in the $325 million range), to foray in on our own made no sense at all."

At the same time, Martin realized, "There are market forces out there that require the use of the Internet from an information and efficiency point of view rather than selling." He also foresaw the power that the established Action Performance collector base, brands, and licensing agreements could bring to a strategic alliance. Thus in a relatively short time, he helped Action Performance develop *three Internet-based initiatives*.

Corporate Accounts

One of these efforts focuses on sales of race car logo merchandise to corporate accounts. As Martin says, "When corporations sponsor race cars, they want hats, shirts and jackets with logos. Often we are the ones who have exclusive licenses with the drivers, so we

Figure 10.1: The Action Performance Web site (www.action-performance.com) promotes the company's lines, licenses and events but does not focus on e-commerce.

Figure 10.2: Action Performance's joint venture with QVC manifests itself in this highly segmented e-commerce site, www.qvc.com/goracing.html as well as QVC's show selling Action Performance products, "For Race Fans Only."

supply that product. These large companies require that you have interactive communications with their purchasing departments so that they don't have to use a printed catalog. They want to see online what's available. So we now have programs that allow you to pick out a shirt, jacket or other item and 'turn it around' online to see the back. Corporations can order completely online—no paper involved—with our system."

Distributor Communications

The second initiative fosters distributor communications. As Martin says, "Many of the sports collectibles retailers have set up their own Web sites because their customers wanted to order that way rather than by phone or in person. We needed to be able to communication about product and descriptions to these distributors."

A Strategic Alliance: The Marriage of QVC and goracing.com

The most prominent of Martin's Internet initiatives for Action Performance involves the firm's relationship with QVC. When Martin arrived at the firm, its executives had already started working with the cable home shopping giant for fulfillment of its collectible club products. Martin explains, "Our members get a catalog each month saying, 'these are the new cars, and you can order them via a toll-free number or on our Web site.' The whole theory is that at least one Thursday a month, a very hot model car will be introduced for the first time. There are only 3,000 of each new car, and if it's really hot, 40,000 people will try to buy it.

"Getting through the phone lines is difficult, but ordering via Internet is not difficult for the collector. Action Performance had set up expensive technology that would allow people to order via Internet, but it was much more cost-effective to outsource the whole fulfillment to QVC—a great organization with much human and technical capital. A company our size can't afford the software costs of data mining and customer tracking and all that. That is one of the benefits of dealing with a company like QVC with its multi-million-dollar data mining software."

The transition to QVC fulfillment had to take place in stages, according to Martin. "First they took over all but the Internet function because the spike that took place on 'big Thursdays' was such that even iQVC (the QVC Web presence) couldn't cover it. It took them awhile to deal with that but now they can handle it."

Seeing how well the QVC relationship was going, Martin and his team went back to QVC and said, "You guys have such great technical capability here—why don't we do something with goracing.com?" As Martin continues, "That was very exciting to QVC, and for our part, we needed to create a national retail presence. Many of our distributors are becoming national on their own via their Web sites, but we wanted our own 'footprint' so that people would know where to get Action Performance products."

TV Home Shopping Converges
with goracing.com

QVC has a show called "For Race Fans Only," which Martin says is the only program the cable channel has ever created "where people tune in on purpose." He explains that QVC sells a great deal of Action Performance product during that one-hour show, but that the hour ends with pent-up demand. "For QVC the question was, 'what do you do with that demand other than wait until next week?'" Martin notes. "Even though iQVC is run very well, racing guys don't want to go to a site that's dominated by jewelry and flowers and the like. Thus the goracing.com alliance made great sense to QVC. They are merchandisers, and we have the name."

QVC and Action Performance struck an agreement where the goracing.com URL would be licensed to QVC for 10 years. QVC took on the expense of getting the site back up and running, and did the merchandising. At the same time, they re-named their NASCAR show "For Race Fans Only—Brought to you by goracing.com." As Martin continues, "They drive traffic to the site, saying if you couldn't get what you wanted tonight, go to the Web site anytime." With millions of race fans nationwide watching the "For Race Fans Only" program during the NASCAR season, traffic to goracing.com is thus assured. QVC took on the fulfillment of Action Performance die cast products, while Action Performance has retained fulfillment of clothing. The firms have worked together so, as Martin puts it, "If someone buys a hat and a model as part of the same order, it looks like it came from the same place."

QVC is now selling Racing Collectables Club of America (RCCA) memberships, but Action Performance retains ownership of the membership list. The club has more than 200,000 members but only 35,000 or 50,000 or so active participants. "The new RCCA members for the most part have never purchased anything from QVC so this is a great deal for them," Martin says. "There was only an 8 percent overlap between our customer base and the QVC base when we began the relationship. As for the customers who utilize goracing.com, that customer list is owned by QVC because it's integrated into their total customer database. Action Performance can use that entire list under mutually agreeable situations."

The QVC alliance has been a true "win-win," and also has been instrumental in upgrading Action Performance's prospects in the financial community. As Martin notes, "Wall Street had concerns about how Action Performance would get people to use the old goracing.com portal site, how high the cost would be to generate that traffic, and how we would fulfill. With the new QVC deal, we have the answers to all those questions. And, when we outsourced to QVC, we became instantly profitable through the Internet channel because all the heavy fixed costs were converted to variable costs so you can't lose money."

Integrating the Web with Other Thriving Channels

Action Performance has never had major problems with its traditional channels of distribution, so now that its Web presence is under control, its trackside, dealer and retail efforts can continue to thrive. A natural for major product sales is the firm's trackside presence at all major NASCAR events. As Martin describes,

> We have 28 long-haul trailers that are painted for individual drivers with their car, colors, pictures and name. Each trailer opens up with a hydraulic system so you effectively have a traveling retail store. It's expensive, but people who go to races have every expectation that they'll be able to find their favorite driver's 'store' there, filled with product. Trackside sales for 2001 were well over $50 million. The margins are high and the prices are similar to those for t-shirts at rock concerts. We have a series of vehicles that go out on the road during the week to re-stock the trailers, sort of like supplying an army. One July weekend at Pocono we sold $1.5 million—and that was just a mid-tier race. At Las Vegas we sell $3.5 million in a weekend.

Action Performance also has 17 distributors that sell to between 8,000 and 10,000 dealers. "Some dealers are small, in strip malls with 2,000 square feet or so," Martin says. "Some are larger." When Action Performance launches a program for a new collectible car, they tell distributors, who get pre-orders from dealers. Then Action Performance sets a strict limit on the amount of product that will be made. When the product comes in, the dealers have already determined the quantities they will get. By contrast, apparel is made in advance and sold out of inventory as distributors, corporations or trackside demand dictate.

The final major channel for Action Performance is mass retail, such as Wal-Mart and K-Mart. As Martin explains, "The big retailers mainly sell the smaller model cars, hats and t-shirts. There aren't very many NASCAR/Winston Cup tracks, so if you don't travel to the races or live near one of the tracks, you can't buy trackside. The specialized dealers have traditionally sold to hard-core race fans. If you're not a hard-core fan, you'd be more likely to purchase your NASCAR product at Wal-Mart or K-Mart."

Tight Controls Foster the Turnaround

As successful as Action Performance's online marketing initiatives have been, having a seasoned CPA at the financial helm was also crucial. Unlike some of the failed dot.coms, Action Performance now has an executive who comfortably "speaks the language" of the financial community and enjoys long-established credibility with its opinion leaders. "I still talk to about 10 institutions and two analysts a day," Martin says. In his early weeks with the company, Martin was able to head off many of the rumors at a time when as he says, "the 'shorts' were after the company." As he explains, "In its natural form, a decision to sell short is just like a decision to buy long—it's an investment based on the situation. You do get 'shorts' who go out and create problems to try to force the price down. This company had its share of 'shorts' out there creating rumors that may have had some attachment to reality, but the implications did not."

By December of 2000, Martin and his team "knew we had plugged the holes." They struck the initial deal for QVC outsourcing and cut back on expenditures. Then they made some difficult decisions that had to do with the culture of Action Performance. "We let 97 people go from a call center here in Phoenix," Martin recalls. "Fred Wagenhals viewed the call center as the 'community' of the RCCA. When somebody called up they didn't just buy a model car, they'd talk about the latest race. Collectors had their favorite call center guy. Our call center people would love to talk for 10 minutes about racing and then sell two cars. At QVC they don't do that. They just sell cars. That transition was difficult. Fred considers it a problem and it makes him feel bad. He gets letters all the time from people saying 'these QVC people don't even know anything about NASCAR.' The call center we had was more than orders and shipping documents. It's not that way any longer, but the 'QVC way' makes money for the business."

Martin also started the process of retiring a total of $40 million in debt between September 2000 and June 2001. He even insisted on signing every check for the entire company to make sure there were no unnecessary financial drains. "In January it became apparent to the market that we were turning around," he says. "We had a break-even first quarter 2001 even with very low revenues—that's not our season. Investors who were out there bottom-fishing and had done their homework were buying ACTN."

Looking back on a roller-coaster year, Martin summarizes what he and Action Performance have learned. "It seems to me that the whole Internet marketing issue is related to technical capability—both merchandising and IT—and the ability to attract people to your Web site who come for reasons other than bargains. I think it's very difficult for a company of our size to compete effectively without a unique formula. In this case, we got lucky and found it through our strategic partnership with QVC. I'm kind of a 'belt and suspenders' kind of guy, so I hate to spend money. If we can't drive revenue through an expenditure, then I won't allocate the dollars. That simple reality wasn't focused on in the late 1990s because there were more grandiose things to think about with the dot.coms. But if you fully allocate your expenses and do what it takes to drive revenue, you *can* succeed online."

Chapter Recap:

- Action Performance reassessed its Web marketing position and helped ensure its viability as a public company by:
    —Entering a strategic and synergistic partnership with QVC that allowed the firm to eliminate the costly overhead of its own online selling presence.
    —Integrating the Web with other thriving channels: trackside, dealer, retail and club.
    —Tight cost controls.
    —Constant, open communication with market analysts.

11 | American Blind and Wallpaper Factory: Making Shopping Fun
www.decoratetoday.com

Most everyone dreams of a tastefully decorated home with stylish window treatments, wallpaper, paint, and artwork that expresses their individuality. But according to Steve Katzman, CEO of American Blind and Wallpaper Factory, customers dread selecting these items. "The average home décor customer has 2.5 children, goes to between three and five retail stores, and spends an hour to two hours in each store flipping through heavy, unwieldy wallpaper books," Katzman reveals. "In focus groups, customers tell us they hate this process." Yet since most households can't or won't pay a professional decorator, they used to believe they had no other choice.

Katzman finds that such customers are delighted to discover his company's Web site. They may get there in response to one of his ubiquitous lead generation spots on cable or his small-space ads in the back of shelter publications. The firm's print catalogs drive traffic to decoratetoday.com as well. "Customers use our Web site to bypass the traditional methods of buying blinds, wallpaper and other such products. They want us to make it fun," he believes. "They also want us to provide someone knowledgeable to help them at no extra charge—someone who will fulfill their needs rather than trying to 'sell' them on the special of the week."

The "always on" aspect of Web buying also appeals to these customers. "We offer 24-hour-a-day phone service and live chat," Katzman says. COO Dan Gilmartin adds, "Our online selection is huge. We have put over 250,000 wallpaper images on the Web as well as the ability to search easily. Including blinds and other product lines, our site presents 500,000 total images. That saves the customer a great deal of time going from place to place to look for the items they want."

Gilmartin acknowledges that customers like to touch and feel home decor products before making their selections. "So we'll send them samples of whatever they want to see," he explains. American Blind and Wallpaper Factory prepares and ships special boxes with generously sized pieces that show off the colors, textures and patterns of blinds, wallpapers and paint chips. The boxes are prepared for a nominal charge that is refunded with a customer's purchase.

A Sticky Site That's Fun for Home Decorators

From the comfort and privacy of home—or during lunch hours or breaks at work—American Blind and Wallpaper Factory customers enjoy both the power and fun of the decoratetoday.com Web site. Instead of flipping through wallpaper books endlessly, customers can use drop-down menus to seek patterns on scores of themes. Or as Katzman says:

Figure 11.1: At www.decoratetoday.com, American Blind and Wallpaper Factory offers tens of thousands of home décor products including wallpaper, blinds, wall art, rugs and accessories.

Figure 11.2: American Blind and Wallpaper Factory customers may select wall art and then change to a variety of matting, frames and background colors with the click of a mouse. Similar options are available for customers comparing wallpaper patterns and coordinating paint colors.

Figure 11.3: Mrs. Kay's, a retail chain of wallpaper and blind stores, has evolved into American Blind and Wallpaper Factory and www.decoratetoday.com under the leadership of Steve Katzman and his executive team.

Figure 11.4: American Blind and Wallpaper Factory still has two complete showrooms in the Detroit area, where customers can shop in a retail environment and the firm's telephone and online sales representatives can be trained.

Figure 11.5: American Blind and Wallpaper Factory's paper catalog is used to fulfill inquiries from television, the Web and other sources and is mailed to the firm's customers and prospects.

If you are looking for a pattern that combines images of kittens, tulips and butterflies, you can put that into our search function and drill down to those specific papers. We have a huge commitment to color and functionality.

You can view paint colors that go best with the wallpapers you choose as well—we'll offer five suggestions or you can use our color chart to make your own paint selections. We're also building a function that will say, 'People who have bought this wallpaper have also bought this border, or paint, or other related products.' Most people are looking for someone to help them make a decision.

The site offers a wide variety of wall art with many entertaining options. Site visitors can combine their favorite images with any number of matting and frame styles, and the customized image pops up immediately. Wondering how that picture will look on your buttercup-yellow wall? Just select the background color of your choice and the artwork will appear on it immediately for your approval.

Site visitors can set up their own online scrapbooks with folders for various rooms they're decorating and go back to change and update them using password-protected access. Many customers take advantage of the option to e-mail images to friends and family members to get their input. "We'll be adding to the scrapbook function to show all the items you've selected in a three-dimensional room setting," Katzman says. "We haven't even scratched the surface yet on cross-promotional activities."

When customers are stumped or want some assistance from a knowledgeable source, they can access Personal Shopper. Katzman explains, "You describe what you are looking for and within 24 hours we respond. We process 1,000 of these requests each day for people who either can't figure out how to use the site or just don't have time. This is one-to-one marketing to the nth degree. We have dedicated people to answer these questions. They take specific training in addition to what they learn to work in our call center. The training program for the sales group is three weeks long. It's interactive; you learn to do a certain function and then practice in our retail store for a few days. Then you come back to learn more."

From Retail to Phone to Internet

While American Blind and Wallpaper Factory now has only two Detroit-area retail outlets, it evolved from a Katzman family-owned business that once included 32 Midwestern stores. "The first store opened about 50 years ago, and they were called Kay and Kay Tile and Wood Paneling Center" Steve Katzman explains. "Then in the late 1980s we opened 'Mrs. Kay's Wallpaper, Blinds and More.' We saw the business evolving as customers starting calling around to get the best price on specific items. We have followed the customer's lead and the changing landscape of retail, staying on the cutting edge. First we moved to a shop-at-home format based on toll-free calling. Then in 1996 we added our Internet presence in response to the customer's desires."

Katzman continues, "We're the Burger King of the home decorating industry. 'Have it your way' is our motto. Whatever way you want to communicate with us, we'll do it. It costs too much to have a customer consider working with you to shut them out. For instance, I think Amazon.com is leaving a ton on the table by not taking phone orders. They'll take phone calls and answer every question, but won't accept an order on the phone. To me that's insane. We have always been very focused on making it easy for consumers to communicate back and forth."

Moving online to serve customers has clearly paid off for Katzman and his company. As he reports, "We have gone on record as selling tens of millions of dollars on the Web. Most exciting of all, a full 60 to 70 percent of that is completely incremental, representing customers we didn't have at retail or on the phone."

Average order size online is higher than the offline average. The lifetime value of Web customers is a little higher and their frequency is higher as well, according to Katzman: "We are segmenting Web buyers out in terms of ongoing investment. You have to market to them differently. There are different things that motivate the Web customer to buy. It's not price, which was the traditional motivator for our offline customers. Online buyers expect a strong guarantee, and payment terms such as 90 days same as cash. We facilitate this by letting people apply for our house charge online with quick approval."

Instant Responsiveness to Customer Feedback

The American Blind and Wallpaper Factory site is constantly under tune-up and revision. As Katzman explains, "We make functional changes almost every day to enhance the consumer experience and help increase conversion rates." Throughout the site, customers are offered the opportunity to respond to short online surveys. The firm receives about 500 to 600 of these surveys per week, according to Dan Gilmartin. When surveys offer constructive criticism that makes intuitive sense, the team acts immediately to implement changes. For example, at one time a site search for wallpaper brought up 6 images per page. Now up to 15 views appear at once, and each can be clicked on twice to make them bigger. This change came from consumer feedback on surveys.

The firm also conducts extensive focus groups at least twice per year and "measures everything," aiming to increase sales per user session, according to Katzman. What's more, they keep careful track of time of site access and method of access. "We get a lot of traffic from work during the day and from 56K modems at home," he reports. This has implications for download times and site efficiency: not everyone is logging on with a high-speed connection.

Both Katzman and Gilmartin clearly relish using their firm's highly functional back-end tools—both for the Web and for other media. Sitting in the company conference room or their own offices, they can listen in to real-time sales and customer service phone conversations from their onsite call center. This includes calls generated specifically from the dedicated toll-free number on the Web site. They can also check call records based on sales rep, call subject, length, results and other measures. They can click on any archived call and listen to a recording of it, as well.

Both executives also tap into the e-mail stream frequently. "It's not unusual for Steve or me to respond to a question personally," Gilmartin says. "We get a ton of feedback that way. If there is a theme in the phone calls or e-mails, whether positive or negative, we will react to it promptly. In addition, our management team gets together and listens to customer service and sales calls weekly." Katzman concludes, "Someday we may well get into more nuances of testing and navigational issues. But for now there's still plenty of low-hanging fruit for us to use in enhancing our site based on the in-house methods we've employed."

Chapter Recap:

- American Blind and Wallpaper Factory's Web site makes what was traditionally a chore into a low-stress, enjoyable, at-home or lunch hour experience.
  —An extensive search engine replaces flipping through scores of heavy wallpaper books and walking through aisles of window treatments and paint cans.

—Scrapbook feature lets customers build, revise and share decor plans.

—Functional site allows visitors to combine backgrounds and colors to accurately visualize room decor and accessories.

- The firm has evolved from retail to phone to Internet as customer needs and preferences changed.
- The firm places a high value on back-end functionality and exceptional online and off-line customer service from well-trained personnel.

Carnival Cruise Lines: Online Sales Are Not Always the Goal

12

www.carnival.com

With the growing prominence of Travelocity, Expedia, Priceline and other "do-it-yourself" travel options online, many Internet prognosticators have predicted the death of the traditional travel agency. Indeed, when www.carnival.com was first launched in 1996, the firm had a goal of booking cruises direct-to-consumer online. But while a self-service site may fill the bill for straightforward hotel or airline bookings, many travelers still crave face-to-face guidance for discretionary, personal travel—especially packaged trips and cruises. That's why even though Carnival Cruise Lines has developed a handsome and robust Web site, the firm currently sees itself in a supporting role online, not as a direct seller to consumers.

"Carnival Cruise Lines is principally a business-to-business marketer of cruises through travel agents," says the firm's e-commerce marketing director, Diana Rodriguez-Velazquez. "About 90 percent of our bookings are made through these agents, facilitated by our 65-person sales force. We do get some business directly through on-line travel partners like Expedia, but currently only a minuscule number of bookings take place at www.carnival.com."

Having prospects surf the Carnival Web site before sitting down with their travel agents or speaking with a phone rep smoothes the way to the sale, according to Rodriguez-Velazquez. "Cruise booking is a highly considered purchase. The Internet provides an ability for the consumer to learn more about options that are available to them. It provides an opportunity to overcome objections or concerns such as the amount of activities available during a cruise, shipboard security, timing, itineraries and the like."

Even so, customers enjoy greater satisfaction when purchasing through telemarketing or a travel agent. "The rep can answer questions, address concerns, and trade the customer up to better cabins, service, side trips, and so on," says Rodriguez-Velazquez. Leads obtained on the Internet are followed up by Carnival outbound telemarketing staff for this purpose. The site invites prospects to fill out a simple form and have a Personal Vacation Planner contact them.

Carnival's greatest success online, according to Rodriguez-Velazquez, has been in terms of increasing communications with the traveler. In the past, she says, travel agents have been wary about giving Carnival the actual names of travelers for fear that Carnival will try to take on the primary client relationship. "Traditionally, Carnival doesn't have an opportunity to provide information directly to the customer until the tickets are processed—only a week or two before the trip," she explains. But now that many travelers spend time online researching and dreaming about their cruises, Carnival can harvest a wealth of information about customer interests, profiles and much more.

Figure 12.1: At www.carnival.com, prospects and customers explore the fun and options available to them on Carnival cruises. Then they are encouraged to speak directly with a sales representative to book their vacations.

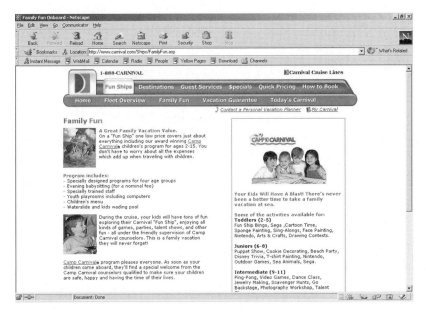

Figure 12.2: Carnival's Family Fun page shows parents and children all the activities and child care that will be available to them on a family cruise.

MyCarnival Serves Customer Needs and Tracks Their Interests

The Carnival Web site invites prospects to set up their own MyCarnival accounts simply by specifying a login and password and providing some basic information, including address, phone, e-mail, date of birth, desired travel dates, trip duration and destination. Thus, as Rodriguez-Velazquez notes, "The Internet offers an opportunity for us to track what interests the consumer—for instance, do they prefer Alaska, the Caribbean, or another location." These interests can also be related to age and other demographics—information that is helpful in selecting other promotional methods and media. The site also captures number of unique visitors, length of sessions, number of repeat visitors, and number of registrations for e-mail newsletters.

Once a customer sets up a MyCarnival account, she can use it to bookmark possible cruise choices and other pages of interest within the site. MyCarnival also facilitates customer research and bookings, and sending of online eCards—a clever form of viral marketing. The eCards picture Carnival ships and exotic locales and allow the sender to personalize the message. The recipient gets an e-mail inviting him to paste a specific URL into his browser. The image that pops up looks like a regular, mailed postcard, but it's framed by the site menu of the Carnival Web site. The recipient can click onto "destinations," "pricing," "specials," "group travel" and much more right from the card's pick-up URL.

Through MyCarnival, the Web site also provides for an additional profit center for Carnival, one that does allow the firm to sell directly to consumers and their family and friends. Click on the button for Gifts and Services, and an array of going-away gifts appears. These can be ordered online for a friend or loved one going on a cruise, or as a treat for oneself. Selections include photo coupons, bar coupons, stateroom decorations, birthday or anniversary specialties, wine and champagne, flowers, food, Carnival merchandise, and shipboard credits. Another profit center is the Carnival Master Card, an affinity credit card that allows its holders to finance a Carnival vacation and earn discounts and upgrades through Fun Rewards points.

Site Evolution Focuses on Content Development

Because of the Internet's support function for Carnival Cruise Lines, Rodriguez-Velazquez says that "the site has been expanded to offer more content to assist the purchase decision—enough information to sell the trip, but not book it. The evolution of the site to date has been focused on adding content, not on how to make booking simple." One prominent example is the site's colorful and fun Camp Carnival section, aimed at enticing children and families to consider a Carnival cruise. Camp Carnival features games, examples of kids' cruise activities, interactive puzzles, virtual tours of kids' favorite parts of the ship, and more.

On another section of the Web site, visitors can download pictures of each of Carnival's 16 ships or a 3-D image of Carny, the carnival.com mascot. A section for first-time cruisers addresses a novice's concerns and assures prospects that no matter what their age or stage of life, there's a Carnival cruise for them. There is also a FAQ section that can be accessed by key words or through a pull-down menu. For those who want to learn more about the ships and their activities, the site offers deck plans and photos of staterooms and public areas as well as schedules for typical morning, noon and nighttime events. The destinations section tells about ports of call, tours, golf packages and other off-ship diversions.

Under development is a system that will allow Carnival to create a recommendation profile similar to those available at amazon.com when travelers revisit the site—based on what the customer reveals in his or her sign-up information for MyCarnival. There will also be chat boards available for travelers to share their questions and experiences with fellow cruisers.

According to Rodriguez-Velazquez, at this point only 11 percent of American households have participated in one or more cruises, so the opportunity to provide novices with interactive, engaging information makes online marketing very valuable to Carnival. What's more, she says, "The Internet is potentially more powerful than other channels in that only online can you truly interact with a brand. If rich content is provided, a visitor can peruse features which are pertinent to their decision making. Given the right presentation of features and benefits—a prospect is much more likely not to be off-sold when visiting a third party. That's powerful."

Chapter Recap:

- Carnival provides support for travel agents, prospects and customers rather than focusing on selling directly online.
- MyCarnival serves customer needs and tracks their interests.
- Site evolution focuses on developing rich content aimed both at prospects and their children.
- The goal of carnival.com is to allow customers and prospects to "interact with the brand" and discover Carnival Cruise Lines' many features and benefits.

13 CDW/CDWG: The Personal Touch
www.cdw.com and
www.cdwg.com

"Seventy percent of our sales come from customers who use our Web site to educate themselves but then may use traditional means—calling an account manager—to place an order," says Jim Shanks, President of CDW Government, Inc. (CDWG) and Executive Vice-President of CDW. "The original strength of the Internet for us has been providing our customers with opportunities for research and education."

Because the computers and related products that CDW and CDWG sell are quite complex, Shanks says, "The Internet gives us a great canvas to take that information and structure it so people can understand. Side-by-side comparisons are quite powerful. We deal with virtually all manufacturers, so we can put all the different brands next to each other and show you a grid of features, plus associated pricing. We help synthesize the information so you can make a valid business decision. We've found that computer products are ideal for the Internet."

Shanks points out that CDW has a competitive advantage over other direct marketers because it sells many major brands. "What we do is explain the advantages of each brand. It's o.k. for us to make comparisons among brands, but we don't get into recommendations." This impartial approach builds CDW's credibility among buyers and vendors alike.

What's more, as President of CDW's government and educational subsidiary, CDWG, Shanks has been able to provide both faster service and more customization than his competitors can offer. "The government had their way of doing business, and everyone was going after the big order—the big government contract. The process took months and was very complex. What the Internet provided us on the "G" side was the opportunity to shorten those cycles. Once we win a contract, we can build a customized, password-protected procurement system for governmental agencies. It can be used for years to see that entity's whole purchase history. Also, we can execute on the small orders—even one or two PCs at a time. It doesn't have to be a $500,000 order. The Internet is really helping the government become more efficient in buying, and we're a big part of that."

Having two sophisticated, high-traffic Web sites also has enabled CDW/CDWG to double the benefits of online enhancements, Shanks reveals. "The Web sites of CDW and CDWG are updated constantly, but one changes before the other. One launches with a new look and feel, they get customer feedback, and then we move the other site forward to pick up the enhancements that work the best."

Figure 13.1: The www.cdw.com site features Resource and Product Finder indexes on the left side and featured products and offers on the rest of the home page.

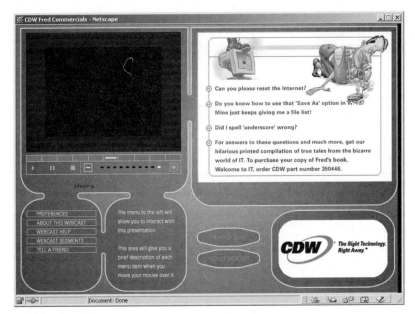

Figure 13.2: IT personnel get a kick out of CDW's humorous "Fred" TV commercials, and they can watch some of the current crop right on the Web site.

Figure 13.3: At www.cdwg.com, CDWG provides customized products and services for government and education buyers.

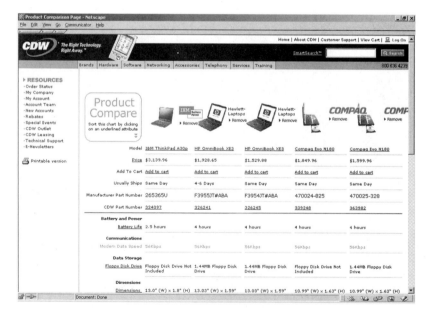

Figure 13.4: CDW's Web site allows customers to compare various computers they are considering on the basis of price, power, dimensions and other features.

An Online Veteran Reaps the Rewards of Foresight

Even before the World Wide Web gained mass acceptance among businesses, CDW was using the Internet to educate its buyers. "Our success is consistency since 1995," Shanks says. "Our IT department created our first Web site with information posted so people could see and learn about our products. The next evolution was to allow for ordering online in 1996."

Many traditional firms have suffered channel conflict when they start selling online, due to poor planning or lack of insight into customers and employees. On the other hand, CDW realized early that the personal touch would still be essential in selling complex, high-ticket items like computers. As Shanks explains,

> We did one very smart thing: We continued to compensate the account managers. Some firms thought they would save money by not paying commission to salespeople for online purchases. We still assign every account to an account manager and pay them commission. This helps to build lasting relationships with our customers.
>
> Each of our customers has someone who already has 'skin in the game' here at CDW. For the newer account managers, we help them build their account base. If you have bought directly from an account manager in the past and now come on the Web, we recognize that and get the information back to the correct account manager—the assigned account manager you have bought from before. We spend as much time marketing internally about the Internet and e-commerce as we do externally. As a result, our account managers are the biggest advocates of the Web site in the company. We continue to communicate the Web site's benefits to our account managers and in turn, they communicate the benefits to our customers.

That personal touch extends to the evolution of the CDW Web site as well. As Shanks notes, "We update our Web site based on a very simple strategy—listen to your customers. We get many e-mails and notes from customers suggesting changes. A lot of firms have been hurt by 'chasing the gadget' (putting 'cool' functions online that slow customers down or don't facilitate their needs). But you have to look at your customer set before adding anything to the site and ask yourself, 'Will that play out?'"

As an example, Shanks notes that suggestive selling often works beautifully in the consumer environment, "But on a B-to-B technology site it isn't as valuable because people tend to be very unique in their combination of devices. We give them all the information but don't try to impose value judgments. When customers call us they have a pretty good idea of what they want to buy. We do associative selling such as toner with copiers, suggesting more memory for computers and the like. But we don't go to the extent of the consumer side—that tends to annoy business customers."

CDW Integrated its Channels from "Day One" Online

Shanks is grateful for many of the marketing decisions he and his colleagues made intuitively in the mid-1990s, as they have helped avoid many pitfalls suffered by traditional direct marketers and dot.coms online. "From the very beginning, we looked at our numbers and saw the impact of our catalog working with the Web site. We have never looked at the Internet in isolation. The power came from the combination of the catalog, Web, general advertising and phone—having everything working in unison and benefiting from the synergy of traditional and new marketing channels.

"To enhance our traditional catalog channel, we have 'magalogs,' which combine editorial material at the front with a catalog at the back. The magalogs include interviews with some of the top people from our vendor firms. Our customers are becoming more sophisticated. They not only want to understand product but also what's going on in the marketplace and the industry. It's great for our credibility to have exclusive information from these movers and shakers. It helps us to become a full business solution."

Because of its size, CDW can afford to use media that other direct and interactive marketers often avoid due to cost. As Shanks notes,

We do TV, and we had an ad campaign that was so popular that countless people wrote in and asked for copies of the spots. So we put them on CD-ROMs and sent them out to people. We had a blimp for a while, and even a plane pulling a sky banner. We've used bus wraps, billboards and radio—we continue to use just about every marketing channel we can think of. Some are more successful than others and some are seasonal. Our 'Buyer's Edge' e-mail newsletters go out to subscribers each week, and they are highly customized. We know Macintosh users don't want to hear about PCs and vice-versa. There are about eight different basic versions of 'Buyers' Edge'.

The media mix continues to fluctuate. At first, the Internet was a very small part of our budget but as we saw its growing importance, we beefed up our advertising campaign there. Driving clicks was never our goal. With every media buy we're looking to drive sales. There were marketers that spent a year or two of big budgets dedicated to banners that yielded zero.

Customer technology seminars are important, too. We bring customers in from all over the country once a month, about a couple hundred at a time. We take them out to dinner, tour the facility and warehouse, and show them our sophistication and automation. The next day we have seminars on technology and bring in a company such as HP to 'get under the covers' of their products.

Shanks says that on the government side, trade shows are key. "We have a 40′ × 40′ booth. We have the biggest, brightest bags. People often look at trade shows as a singular event, but like anything in marketing it needs to have a campaign around it—a theme and consistent follow-up."

E-Commerce and CDW Culture

While Shanks is matter-of-fact about CDW's online growth, he realizes that there's much more than luck and intuition involved. "Our success comes from our culture," he says. "We have a whole list of slogans to live by, including 'Success means never being satisfied,' and 'It's only good if it's win-win.' We're always trying to do things better, not looking at the past but what's on the horizon. We look at what other companies are doing and ask how else could they have done it and what would have worked better."

They also realized early on that the Internet wasn't just a marketing vehicle but also more of a business automation device. It had always "lived in" IT. They did create a Strategic Business Unit (SBU) to have all the different disciplines covered in that group, but the SBUs are charged with staying integrated with the rest of the organization, attending meetings, keeping the look and feel the same, and so on. In keeping with their culture, they do take risks online, do a lot of piloting, and try to deliver what their customers ask for. Sometimes they find that they have to say no to their customers, but they try to find a compromise to fit their needs with something that is scalable.

The SBU has made sure that on the CDW back-end, "everything flows," as Shanks puts it. "Whether an account manager places an order, or whether the customer mails it in, faxes it in, or places it electronically over the Internet, all orders flow into the same system. And we pride ourselves on the fact that everything an account manager can see about an order, the customer also can see for themselves. Traditionally you had to call to enter an order and call to check on it, but today you can order and check the status of your order by yourself if you choose to. You can see where the order is, get shipping information, and anticipated delivery."

Shanks' advice to fellow e-commerce marketers is straightforward. "Determine what you want to be, create a business model that supports it, and stick to it! Measure everything, so that when there's any question you can drill down and come up with an answer very quickly. Don't overanalyze or get preoccupied with the data. Take some risks! It's such a quick feedback loop that you can try things and tell very quickly whether people like it or not. The Internet is an incredible environment for innovation."

Chapter Recap:

- CDW's site focuses on research and education; 70 percent of customers still buy via direct contact with their account managers.
- CDWG provides a segmented site to meet the unique needs of customers in government and education.
- CDW helps avoid channel conflict—and ensures exemplary customer service—by compensating account managers even when their customers buy independently online.
- CDW integrated its channels and marketing communications from "day one" online.
- CDW's online presence is immersed in the company's culture.

14

Chicago Symphony Orchestra: Sophisticated Software

www.cso.org

Whether you're surfing the 'Net from your office near Symphony Center, or planning a Windy City visit from your home in Tokyo, the Chicago Symphony Orchestra Web site lets you choose the exact seats, stage view and price you prefer for any available concert. With its database and Web site software upgrades, CSO's Web page now ranks among the most dynamic in today's entertainment world.

"We've gone through a major revision that lets you pick your seats on a three-dimensional map of the hall," says CSO Director of Marketing, Kevin F. Giglinto. "This will change the way many organizations do ticketing in the future, but the CSO is the first to use this application. It's done through an outside vendor in Atlanta—Intelitix. They're the ones with the engine enabling us to launch this function, with support from our Chicago Web developers, IA Collaborative

Figure 14.1: The Chicago Symphony Orchestra (www.cso.org) Web site's Symphony Store offers visitors from all over the world the opportunity to purchase CDs., books, videos, posters and a host of other licensed products.

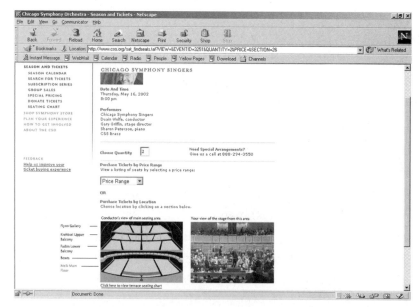

Figure 14.2: Ticker purchasers at the CSO Web site may check various seating and pricing options and view exact seat locations as well as each seating area's view of the stage.

and Lynch ☐ . All three of these vendors have gone 'above and beyond' in working with us, and I couldn't be happier." With the 3-D site scheduled to activate in May of 2002, it's clear that Giglinto is almost as good at "orchestration" as the CSO's famed musical director and conductor, Daniel Barenboim.

Changing Audiences Require Adaptive Customer Relationships

The CSO bills itself as "rich in tradition . . . innovative in vision," with a legacy that extends back to 1891. The orchestra's 110 musicians perform 200 times a year, both in Chicago and throughout the world. Yet like all other classical music organizations today, the symphony must face the fact that its core audience is aging rapidly. Thus the CSO must find ways to attract and retain new and younger audiences. "We're competing with all other methods of live entertainment for the little disposable time that people have," Giglinto notes. "In a way, theater and opera are different, but then again it's all 'Friday night out.' The Internet is the primary growth channel for us."

Even before the 3-D site launched, Giglinto realized that www.cso.org was helping the symphony attract new attendees—at least on an event-by-event basis. He sees at least two reasons for this. First, people who were not brought up with the symphony may be intimidated to call and ask basic questions about ticket protocol, what to wear, and what will be played. "Online, people can get answers for these questions themselves without having to ask someone on the phone or in person."

Second, the Web site has been designed for an easy interface and quick ticket buying. "Our average visitor spends just nine minutes on the site. Overwhelmingly they search for an event, buy some seats and get off. It's 'self-serve'—and it's the way people are coming to the symphony for the first time," he says. Indeed, Giglinto says that a full 70 percent of people who bought symphony tickets online during the 2000–2001 season were not in the organization's database. "They might have been walk-ups previously, but that still says quite a bit about the power of the Web site."

The next challenge for www.cso.org will be to provide a comfort level for newer, online buyers to facilitates their purchase of subscription tickets online. "The majority of our performances are sold on a subscription basis," Giglinto says, "which is a pretty hefty purchase—typically $450 per person, or $900 to $1000 for a couple, to attend a five to 10-series package. You need to become engaged with customers to get that level of commitment online." Of $25 million in total annual ticket sales for the CSO, between $15 and $17 million are subscription sales.

According to Giglinto, Customer Relationship Management will be the key to reaching the level of customer confidence needed for subscription purchasing online. "Our new 3-D system coordinates the same live inventory whether you are phoning, faxing, mailing or going online to buy subscriptions or tickets. The challenge in the past was that the systems that were available for selling online restricted us to only certain blocks of seats. At that point we were allocating seats by source—so you'd be offered different options depending on the medium you used." In addition to streamlined subscription purchasing online, the relaunch also offers a "quick click" renewal option for past subscribers. "That eliminates a lot of the burden for our phone sales," Giglinto notes.

In the interest of symphony patrons, Giglinto also insisted that the new database system handle merchandise and tickets in the same online shopping cart. "Most vendors couldn't promise that. We persevered until we found one that could," he says. Online sales of merchandised doubled between 1999–2000 and 2000–2001, with another impressive increase expected now that 50 additional items have been added.

Pleased with the results of the relaunches he's supervised, Giglinto comments, "What I would say to other orchestras is that you get what you pay for, and sometimes it's worth the capital investment to make it as easy as possible for people to buy. A lot of other orchestras have used a developer called Pegasus that produces what I call cookie-cutter sites with cookie-cutter functionality. I figure that our new system puts us about two years ahead of most major arts groups."

Early Success Fueled CSO
Online Investment and Integration

While the percentage of total CSO ticket sales generated online is still relatively modest, the organization's leadership has seen such dramatic reactions to Web site improvements and integration that they have willingly made the investments Giglinto advocates. When the CSO site first went live with selling capabilities, "We tripled the traffic we had at the site because it became ubiquitous in all our promotions. Our print media really drive traffic to the 'Net, whether by ads or direct mail. We even have banners on our building featuring the URL—they're seen by passersby and people on public transportation."

To facilitate this integration, the CSO's print creative director was involved in the front-end Web site design so it has the same look and feel as the group's other media. "We use the same fonts, and the same imagery and photography both online and offline," Giglinto notes. "We kept a simple color scheme online—we didn't want color to get in the way of the information and ordering. That's also a look we have been using for some of our brochures."

The integration efforts have paid off handsomely on the CSO's financial statement, Giglinto reveals. "Sales online have been fantastic. In fact, we quadrupled online sales when we upgraded from a relatively insecure, simple order form to one designed to make it easy and secure to buy." That initial site, which mostly served public relations purposes for the CSO, sold $200,000 worth of tickets in 1999–2000, while the upgraded site for 2000–2001 sold $880,000 in tickets. The goal for 2002–2003 is $1.2 million in online ticket sales, plus driving 20 percent of returning customers to renew their subscriptions online in 2003–2004.

As for the relative importance of the media in the current mix, Giglinto comments:

> Direct mail is our number-one sales medium with phone a very close second. But the Internet is coming in pretty close behind phone sales now and it's by far the fastest growing. We have to continue to make it easier and more reliable for people to go online because online sales help make the cost of sales reasonable—and that helps us keep ticket prices down. But we do want to offer our customers whatever assistance they need. Our ticketing department call center has provided great customer care for people who need support placing an order online. We have a toll-free number just to track what's happening on the Web site, and the only place to get that number is online.

Goals for CSO's Online Future

Now that he has the software in place to allow for sophisticated CRM, Giglinto looks forward to working on a model that will reward customers for their relationship with the symphony. He also plans to continue adding value and benefits for customers and site visitors.

Giglinto has already launched a series of opt-in e-mail lists to provide customers with news on topic areas such as piano music or jazz. "We won't do mass e-mail to everyone who has bought," he promises, "and we don't have a general e-mail newsletter." He prefers to keep e-mail communications sharply targeted and personal.

As time and resources permit, Giglinto continues to add enrichment material to the CSO Web site, even though he knows most customer visits are of the "easy on, easy off" variety. "I'm sure there's a good amount of reference work being done on the site, and I know many students come on regularly and surf around," he notes. "When we get questions that aren't answered on the site, I make sure it goes to our public relations people, and they decide who should respond."

To get some customized data on a nonprofit's budget, Giglinto has engaged academic researchers at Michigan State University and DePaul University to survey the CSO's Web buyers. "We'll find out what things they like or don't like, and what they want see on the site." Part of the survey was done before the recent relaunch, and the rest will be done with customers who have had the opportunity to see the relaunched site features. Giglinto also uses feedback from customer e-mails.

One of the definite upgrades in store for www.cso.org is an enhanced personalization function. "We believe in this and are going to spend a lot of money doing it," Giglinto comments. "Originally it was supposed to be done by February of 2002, but it's more likely to go live in September of 2002." This will allow customers to log in and monitor their accounts, generate their own receipts for donations, and perhaps participate in subscriber forums.

Giglinto's most important challenge moving forward will be to balance rewards for older, long-term customers with perks offered to the newer online buyers. As he explains,

> Our traditional customers have been evaluated according to a lifetime value measurement system based on subscription sales, donation dollars, how long they have been with us, and similar criteria. Nobody is more valuable than those who have been with us for 30 years. But for those who choose the cost-effective, online way to begin a relationship with us, we want to provide them with rewards and encouragement. It may be that we offer online customers free shipping and handling. Once I can start analyzing the data from our new system, I'll be able to determine exactly how much cost savings we're realizing from online buyers—and reward them accordingly.

Chapter Recap:

- Chicago Symphony Orchestra customers now may choose their seats on a unique three-dimensional map.
- Attracting new customers and younger customers are major CSO goals online.
- Customer relationship management is key to raising customer confidence to the extent that they will purchase big-ticket subscriptions online.
- Goals moving forward for CSO's online marketing include:
  —Increased use of segmented, opt-in E-mail and newsletters.
  —Enhanced store personalization.
  —Rewarding customers whose online self-service saves the CSO money.

15 J. C. Whitney: Unlimited Depth of Assortment
www.jcwhitney.com

Ed Bjorncrantz has spent much of his marketing career making tough catalog presentation choices. A veteran of both Sears and J. C. Whitney (and now a partner with The Callahan Group, LLC), Bjorncrantz knows what it's like to have to eliminate products—or cut down their allotment on the page—because of a paper catalog's stringent space limitations. That's one of the main reasons he became an early advocate of the Internet while working as VP-Marketing at the venerable 87-year-old direct marketing firm of J. C. Whitney in Chicago.

Since they promise to provide their customers with "Everything Automotive," J. C. Whitney presents tens of thousands of individual products and parts—far too many to be featured productively in traditional catalog form. "You can't mail a catalog big enough to cover all the parts J. C. Whitney offers," Bjorncrantz notes, envi-

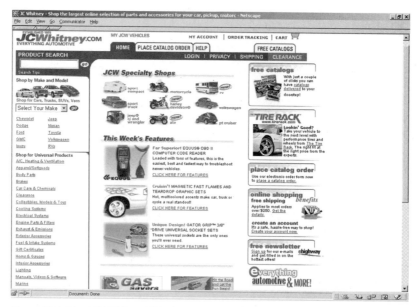

Figure 15.1: The J.C. Whitney Web site at www.jcwhitney.com allows customers to search by vehicle make, product type, or in one of the firm's many specialty shops for motorcycles, Volkswagens, Jeeps and the like.

sioning a tome the size of an urban telephone book. "The firm's general print catalog has over 70,000 part numbers, while the Web site already offers access to over 100,000 potential applications. J. C. Whitney could never cost effectively list all of those in a catalog."

Bjorncrantz acknowledges that building an electronic database of automotive information is very expensive. The search logic behind the online listings is more complex and more extensive than what is available in the paper catalog database, so everything has to be redone from scratch. But once the mechanism is in place, he says, "the incremental cost of listing products online is very low." This major investment is one main reason why J. C. Whitney has little viable competition in the online space. "Our two major upstart competitors online, CarParts and WrenchHead, have both gotten out of the

Figure 15.2: The J.C. Whitney catalog works in synergy with the firm's Web site, providing a powerful reminder to customers and prospects to purchase by mail, phone or online. However, the catalog can hold only a small fraction of the number of products available at www.jcwhitney.com.

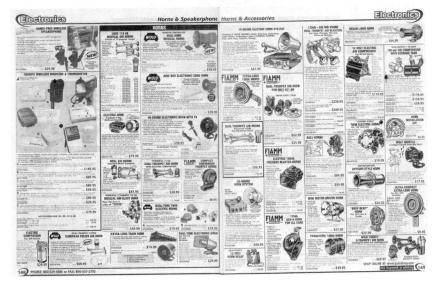

Figure 15.3: Catalog customers may request any one of a number of specialized J.C. Whitney books like this Volkswagen catalog. There is also a Volkswagen icon on the www.jcwhitney.com Web site leading to the same specialized product mix.

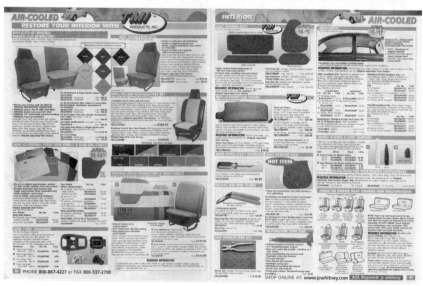

consumer automotive parts business," he says, noting that J.C. Whitney's brand strength is another important factor in its favor. "A well-known brand is extremely important online," Bjorncrantz says. "A recognizable brand gets a lot of search traffic. J. C. Whitney for automotive parts and accessories, Fannie May for candy, Black & Decker for power tools, and so on."

The Luxury of Space for "Delving Deep"

While many items J. C. Whitney stocks are fairly straightforward, Bjorncrantz says he often felt frustrated with the cramped catalog space available to him when he wanted to fully explain the merits of intricate items. At www.jcwhitney.com, however, he says, "You can advertise the item and 'behind it' offer all the details. This allows you to present a complex product line with more support material than you could ever produce in a catalog." The prospective customer can access a great deal of additional information before making a buying decision. "You can profitably carry an item that wouldn't support the advertising space in a catalog."

What's more, after J. C. Whitney went online in 1997, they took the opportunity to extend their product lines, particularly in custom areas. As Bjorncrantz explains, "Search for 'seat covers' on www.jcwhitney.com and you're linked to a vendor's site, transparent to the customer. There are tens of thousands of part numbers at that site, just on seat covers. These are factory ship items. Online the vendor asks all the questions needed to fulfill the order, and the consumer fills in the answers on an online form. The seat covers are then made to order and drop-shipped direct to the customer."

A Fertile Field for Testing

As a career-long direct marketer, Bjorncrantz thrives on testing—and he has found the Internet an ideal medium for controlled experimentation on behalf of J. C. Whitney. "You can test a lot of new items on the Web," he says. "You can introduce products, test pricing, and methods of presentation and promotion online before moving the 'winners' to the paper catalog later.

"The production cycle of the catalog doesn't allow J.C. Whitney to be 'first to market' through the catalog—face-to-face retailers have the advantage over catalog marketers there. But the Internet allows us to supersede retailers. We can have a product up online for testing in a matter of days if we want to. We also have the capacity to deliver alternating presentations on the site either every-other visit, every-other hour, or whatever parameters we set, and we can track conversion and average order size head-to-head on different products, presentations and so on.

"I don't think anybody does enough testing on the Web just like they don't in print media. The test logic has been better established on the mail side. Some of the things we'd like to track we can't, but we can track how many times people are clicking certain features on the home page, and change the site accordingly to try to increase conversion rates, average order size and opt-in e-mail registration and catalog requests."

Bjorncrantz believes there is plenty of work to be done on optimizing online response, and that testing can be very beneficial for this purpose. "You want to eliminate inhibitors to buying, overcome capacity problems, and know where your traffic comes from and who is converting so you can get more of the same. I also advocate increasing targeted promotions such as e-mail, pop-ups, and specialty landing pages or links on the site. Also important are finding ways to reduce the number of steps to buy, and improved customer service."

The Importance of Robust Search Functions

Bjorncrantz advises Internet marketers to invest as much as they can in developing search functions that customers find both intuitive and helpful. He laments the number of prospects J. C. Whitney and other sites lose because site visitors can't figure out how to locate the items they want.

The search function is particularly important for J.C. Whitney because "it's not an impulse-buy company. Customers are looking for a specific product for a specific application. They need to be able to search by product category, by make and model, or by product term. We used a vendor called Creative Good to determine how our customers wanted to search for car parts. Search is critical to successful conversion rates, customer satisfaction and repeats visits. If the customer can't find what they are looking for through keyword search or an easy drill-down, they will leave the site. Once the consumer has a bad experience (search or otherwise) they most likely will not revisit the site."

The Power of Channel Integration

Bjorncrantz says that J. C. Whitney has benefited from today's more realistic environment for online advertising. He says, "Fortunately, Internet advertising is moving in a direction that is to the benefit of the direct marketer. It's more cost per action rather than CPM. A notable holdout is AOL, but you can go to a portal or a site like Ask Jeeves or Overture (formerly GOTO) and pay for click-throughs based on net sales that are generated off of these searches. We want to pay them for the value of their advertising, with a direct way to measure it."

That said, Bjorncrantz believes that the integration of established J. C. Whitney media has been the greatest boon to online traffic and sales. "The catalogs we have out there are tremendous advertising for the Web site—great integration," he comments. "Because of the brand and the tens of million of catalogs J. C. Whitney sends per year, we drove lots of people to the site that would never have gone there otherwise. For other people, the Web site provided a more convenient way to reach us.

"A significant percentage of those who buy on the Web are new to J. C. Whitney. We are generating a lot of new customers with this channel, and doing it cost-effectively. The catalog is still J. C. Whitney's most important marketing tool. It still generates the bulk of the traffic to the site, but the site itself stimulates catalog requests, so they do work in concert. We also place space ads in automotive publications to drive traffic to the Web from young, highly mobile customer segments that are difficult to reach with mail. I would say J. C. Whitney is still primarily a catalog marketer that is offering a second, very supportive complementary online channel."

Bjorncrantz says that online and offline media work synergistically for J. C. Whitney. "The Internet sparks catalog interest and vice-versa. Customers who use both are better customers. Customers can visit the Internet to supplement what they learn from the catalog. You want to make it a similar customer experience. The customer looks at a brand somewhat monolithically. At Sears, a synergy did exist between catalog and retail. Shop the catalog and go to the retail store to touch, feel and buy. Or maybe look at it in the store and go home and buy later from the catalog. We're seeing a similar phenomenon between the catalog and the Web."

To maximize this synergy for J. C. Whitney, Bjorncrantz envisions "a catalog designed for the Internet shopper that provides links to the product on the site." He continues, "In addition, if someone is buying by both Web and mail, ideally you have captured an opted-in e-mail address at one of the points of sale. Then you can use it to promote your catalog and broadcast other targeted messages to that audience. If a customer/requester is mailed a catalog and hasn't responded, an e-mail message can be sent with a special offer or a referral to products of special interest. If you have an e-mail address, it's a very inexpensive way to advise them a catalog is coming, or tell them they just got a catalog and refer them to a promotion, or to stimulate purchases from a catalog that isn't meeting early expected response rates." By the same token, Bjorncrantz notes, the catalog can promote the Web site to try to attract first-time online buyers.

In Hindsight: Lessons Learned

When the Web was young, a number of traditional companies—including J. C. Whitney—made the decision to isolate their fledgling online efforts, either with a separate internal department or an outside vendor. In the mid-1990s, there seemed to be many rational reasons for doing so. Marketers were afraid that internal politics and systems would bog down their efforts to get a viable Web site up and running. But looking back, Bjorncrantz says that J.C. Whitney now must deal with a number of problems dating back to that time. "You pay for the sins later on, but we would never have been up with the time frame that we had set if we tried to integrate the Web totally on the front end. There was a big upside and a big downside to the way we did it.

"The Web business still is not totally integrated with the traditional catalog business, although those limitations are being addressed," he notes. "For example, our call center reps are just now learning how to use the Internet while they talk to the customer. If a customer has a paper catalog, the rep has always been able to see exactly what they are looking at. Once we get all the training and productivity issues ironed out, our reps will be able to do the same when the customer is looking at the Web. We're also working on making it possible for people to buy on the 'Net and then call up to track their orders on the phone. J. C. Whitney customers would like a seamless system, and we're developing efficient systems to deliver that for them."

Now that J. C. Whitney is focused on using Web-based technology where appropriate, the firm's marketing and IT personnel are forging a stronger relationship than ever before, according to Bjorncrantz. "You clearly now have a new level of partnership between marketing and IT. You're faced with integrating merchandising, development, and creative for both online and offline media. IT takes the lead now on upgrading the existing system with the Internet in mind. But the overall lead still has to be marketing because it's still a marketing business."

Chapter Recap:

- The Web offers the potential for "delving deep" and offering nearly unlimited assortment for J. C. Whitney, a firm that bills itself as offering "Everything Automotive."
- J. C. Whitney has found the Web to be a fertile field for testing.
- For a firm with such depth of assortment, a robust internal search engine is vital.
- Online and offline media work synergistically for J. C. Whitney.
- Moving forward, the firm is working toward total integration of its online/offline back end systems.

16

(Mindpepper) Bargainandhaggle.com: Building Relationships Online

www.bargainandhaggle.com

During the late 1990s, American businesses were obsessed with preparing for the possible calamities of Y2K. To help its clients meet the millennial challenge, the CPA firm of BDO Seidman staffed its Grand Rapids, Michigan, headquarters with the best and brightest young information technology stars available. Once Y2K had come and gone, BDO Seidman Chairman Denis Field saw no reason to lose these capable professionals to other firms. He challenged them to think outside the box and come up with a new business plan that would both drive earnings and demonstrate innovation. When the Grand Rapids group developed a unique mechanism for online buying and selling, bargainandhaggle.com and its parent company, Mindpepper, were born.

As former Mindpepper CEO Catherine Ettinger recalls, "At first the idea was just to take bargainandhaggle.com to the point where it

Figure 16.1: Colorful and involving, the bargainandhaggle.com site (www.bargainandhaggle.com) invites customers to buy and sell using the firm's unique one-to-one purchasing concept.

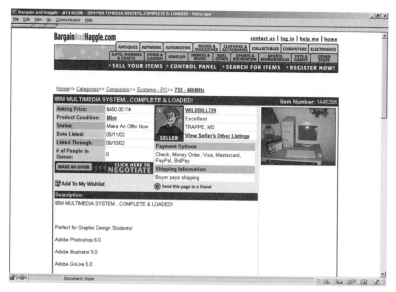

Figure 16.2: Frequent users like WILDBILL729 select their own avatars to present a friendly and engaging persona to prospective customers on bargainandhaggle.com. The top five "producers" are listed on the face of the site so that prospective buyers can click through immediately to their offerings.

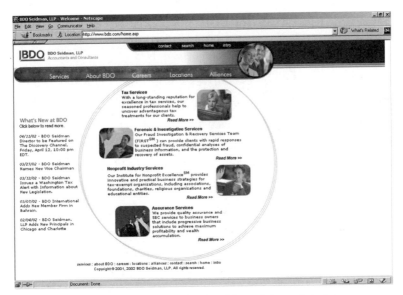

Figure 16.3: Accounting firm BDO Seidman, LLP (www.bdo.com) started bargainandhaggle.com as a part of a division called Mindpeppper. BDO Seidman announced early in 2002 that it would sell bargainandahggle.com to a group of the dot.com's employees.

was paying for itself. That would be a proof of validity for the one-on-one negotiation system the site offers, and then we thought we'd switch our efforts into selling that system to others. Instead, the site itself has just skyrocketed. Once it took that huge leap, Field said he wanted Mindpepper to focus on bargainandhaggle.com as opposed to other products."

By February of 2002, BDO Seidman had concluded that while bargainandhaggle.com was a viable concern, it did not fit with the accounting firm's main business. Thus BDO Seidman opted to dissolve Mindpepper and sell bargainandhaggle.com to a group of the dot.com's employees.

Bargainandhaggle.com
Squares off Against eBay

Ask Ettinger and her top executives whom they regard as their main competition and they answer in unison: "eBay!" Former Mindpepper COO Duncan Maclean says that for bargainandhaggle.com, "eBay is the target. We don't really actively consider uBid and the others. Our big question is always 'what is eBay doing?' We've watched a lot of smaller auction-type sites go out of business."

Maclean and Ettinger believe that eBay is the most viable company on the Internet. Maclean explains, "eBay is successful because they were first, they've done some great marketing, they've developed a really recognizable brand, and they have a business model that works. They are growing aggressively, and they're not afraid to change. They started with Pez dispensers, evolved into collectibles, and then saw the need to move into durable consumer goods. They have had to make business growth decisions that alienate the collectibles consumers. They've been able to ignore the cries because they realize the market is bigger elsewhere. But as they move away from collectibles and toward durable goods, the auction model makes less and less sense. If you have something with intrinsic value, great—that's perfect to be auctioned. But auctions for shoes or for clothes for your kids? An auction for those items is less practical than the one-to-one model on bargainandhaggle.com," Maclean believes.

"Bargainandhaggle.com is a true consumer-to-consumer business with dynamic pricing," Ettinger explains. "It's similar to an auction site because individuals can both buy and sell. What's different is the mechanism by which you are buying or selling. On an auction you are bidding with others and the highest bidder wins. With our negotiated pricing model, you post your items for sale and then an individual comes along and makes you an offer; you negotiate with that individual to strike a bargain. If others come along they are held in an electronic queue until you are done with the first individual. Either party can terminate at any time but if you can strike a bargain, you're done.

"Customers like the aspect of control, the fact that they aren't taking any sort of risk in selling their product, and they don't have to worry about not getting the price they want and having to sell anyway. They also don't have to worry about people who may not really want to buy the item but are just bidding it up. There are also things about our interface that clients really enjoy. We have consistent templates that don't allow for confusing free-form posts. We keep things clean and available 'at a glance.' We have a very straightforward system for getting items, descriptions and photos posted on the site."

Some bargainandhaggle.com sellers use the site to make extra cash, while others consider it a hobby. "Some actually make a living at it," Ettinger adds. Maclean comments, "One of our top users is the wealthy wife of a very successful businessman who does this to keep stimulated. On the other hand, some of our sellers are just scraping by and bargainandhaggle.com helps them make ends meet."

Accountable Media Choices Fuel Customer Growth

Duncan Maclean says that Mindpepper executives originally believed they could attract enough buyers and sellers to their new site through some type of viral marketing campaign. They also tried to build momentum locally through publicity, antique shows, word of mouth and even door-to-door canvassing, but progress was much too slow. "At the beginning we turned down advertising concepts that we thought were too expensive, but now we are spending three times as much as those cost."

The key for Mindpepper was getting away from a CPM model and moving toward "cost per action." They signed a contract with Adtegrity in Grand Rapids to bring prospects to the site. Adtegrity's most successful promotional method for bargainandhaggle.com has been through rented opt-in e-mail lists. "In our first month with Adtegrity, they increased our user base five-fold," Maclean recalls. "From there it doubled every month from January to June 2001 before starting to level off."

Mindpepper's former Marketing Director, Jennifer Jurgens, says that in today's competitive environment, just delivering prospects to the site is not enough. "Our next biggest challenge is to get them to use the Web site. A registered user base doesn't generate revenue. People who act generate revenue. One really good sign is that up to 70 percent of our registered users opt in to receive e-mailed marketing messages about updates and promotions."

At this point bargainandhaggle.com will only pay media sources for customers who register and become active users of the site. For them, the days of CPM, cost per click and other lesser measures are long gone. "If the dot.coms hadn't bombed, we couldn't have done this. Media and list owners would not have accepted our terms," Maclean realizes. "We didn't start this business until the Internet had bottomed out."

Jurgens adds, "I'm a logistics person who now does marketing, so this whole ROI marketing model where we have the data available at a glance is exciting to me. The more we drill into this the better it's going to get. It's fantastic to have immediate feedback on everything we do to promote and sell online. We get what we pay for, always. We can yank unsuccessful things in a matter of hours and that's just incredible. I can't wait to see where it takes us."

Avatars and Rewards Build Trust and Loyalty

Richard G. Barlow, president of Frequency Marketing in Milford, Ohio, defines the function of relationship or "frequency" marketing as follows: "To identify, maintain and increase the yield from best customers through long-term, interactive, value-added relationships." While a formal program with rules and specific benefits and rewards may help fulfill these goals, Web sites like bargainandhaggle.com have gained even more long-term loyalty by combining both formal and informal perquisites based on knowledge of the customer.

To get customers climbing what Jurgens calls "loyalty ladder," she says the first step "is to get people to act three times. We do things like give them five dollars in cash, credit to their credit card or through a payment center once they've met that milestone. We have wonderful loyalty programs. We reward people in tangible ways and they also gain status and stature on the site for doing more. You want the next level if we make it attractive enough."

For many bargainandhaggle.com customers it becomes a matter of pride to move up the scale of what Mindpepper called its "avatar program." Avatars are cartoon representations that let participants remain anonymous—they can be a robot, wizard, or other character—and also customize their selling areas with personal quotes. New users start out at level one and can move up level by level as their volume and credibility increases. The point system rewards participants who are highly rated by fellow customers, and they can also lose points for poor service and performance. Jurgens notes, "You want to have 'level four' or 'level five' show up in your areas on the site so people know you can be trusted and you are a veteran."

The current top five bargainandhaggle.com clients are listed on the face of the page with click-through to their selling areas. This is a much-sought perquisite not only for status reasons but also because of the higher chances that site visitors will click through to see these top sellers' offerings. The higher a client's level, the more benefits he or she receives as well, including free boldface listings, free banner ads, free hats and much more.

Marketing Energizes a
Site Crafted by Bean Counters

Coming out of BDO Seidman, the original bargainandhaggle.com site was "built by accountants," as Catherine Ettinger freely admits. Once the marketer Jennifer Jurgens joined the staff, part of her job was to make the site more inviting, colorful and friendly—another intangible that helps build loyalty. In late 2001, Jurgens and former Information Technology Director Joe Force launched what they call a "1930s-40s-50s look" to announce their five-dollar customer-activation offer. "The site underwent a transition from the look of a black-and-white brochure to something much more personal, 'written' by a cartoon mascot, Mr. Bargainandhaggle," Jurgens explains.

Ettinger realizes that this effort to establish a recognizable look and feel for the site is essential to bargainandhaggle.com's continued growth. "We're already in the top 200 or so sites as far as traffic according to Media Metrics, but we're really just getting started on building a brand," she says. "We have name recognition but no brand equity. We're now easing into who we really are. Our main goal—and the way we make money (based on a cut of final transactions)—is to keep people buying and selling. In order to foster this in a safe, happy place, our site must become more warm and fuzzy."

Chapter Recap:

- Bargainandhaggle.com offers a one-to-one auction model with dynamic pricing that provides buyers and sellers with more control than a conventional online auction.
- After its viral marketing campaign failed, bargainandhaggle.com turned to pay-per-performance ads and e-mails to build its active customer list.
- Avatars and rewards build excitement and loyalty for the site.
- Originally built by accountants, bargainandhaggle.com has become more "warm and fuzzy" to earn trust and increase brand equity.

17 | Omaha Steaks:
An Online Profit Center
www.omahasteaks.com

While flashy and now-defunct dot.coms burned through venture capital money in the late 1990s, Omaha Steaks approached the Internet at its own low-key, steady pace. This solid, Midwestern direct marketing company has always looked for the "smart marketing investment," according to its Senior Vice-President, Todd Simon. "No matter what the medium, you have to have a very clear understanding of your own customer lifetime value model. That lets you understand how much you can spend to acquire a customer. You can't have a sustainable business unless you spend less to acquire customers than their long-term value."

Even so, Omaha Steaks executives were quick to realize the potential of the online medium—and didn't drag their feet getting started. "Our biggest online success is that we didn't overthink it at the beginning," Simon comments. "We got in early and grew the business organically. We made a relatively small investment and learned as we went, building upon that learning. We made and corrected a lot of mistakes that have allowed us to 'back into' a satisfying consumer experience."

Omaha Steaks opened a successful store on Compuserve's electronic mall in 1991 and launched its first Web site in 1995. Simon states:

> At that time we created our own site as well as a store on AOL. The purpose for both was to sell product and provide customer service. Since that time the purpose has not changed, but the functionality has improved tremendously. Now we sell product and also do public relations, have store locators, and offer customer communication mechanisms. Our site has become more robust and has more functionality for consumers, business customers and suppliers alike.
>
> But it's not like we went out and spent a million dollars all at once and then had to do it all over. We've grown our Web business incrementally and cost effectively. For us, and for many traditional catalogers and direct marketers, the Internet is a new front end on an existing business. The great thing is that we can focus it all on the customer experience, not on building new infrastructure. We already had the infrastructure in place, unlike start-up dot.coms. And our strong brand is a real plus. Brand plays a bigger role on the Internet than in other channels because of the level of uncertainty. Online consumers will gravitate toward a strong brand.

New Customers for a New Medium

Simon believes that his customers buy Omaha Steaks for similar reasons no matter what marketing medium they choose. "We have seven points of distinction," he explains. "Grain fed, Midwestern, naturally aged, vacuum sealed, flash frozen, packaging, and reliability. Our product is consistent and consumers know that. Aging meat is an old-world art that is all but lost today, especially at grocery stores. We age our beef for 21 to 28 days before it's cut. That allows for flavor and tenderness you don't find very often these days. Consumers in general are getting over the whole 'fresh versus frozen' thing. We guarantee that ours are going to be the best steaks they've had or we'll give them their money back, so it's risk-free."

Nevertheless, Simon knows that each channel of distribution attracts a distinct type of customer to Omaha Steaks. "The challenge is to have the brand integrated across all channels."

The Internet has introduced a younger consumer to Omaha Steaks, according to Simon. "Initially, that had to do with younger people and men being heavy users of the 'Net," he says. "That's already changing, and our online business will change as women and older people continue to go online." Web buyers offer a significant financial and promotional plus to Omaha Steaks because, as Simon relates, "The ongoing cost of marketing to Web-only customers is significantly lower. That means we can afford to market to them longer without dropping them."

While some firms have endured departmental infighting due to customer migration from other media to the Web, Simon finds there is not a lot of crossover among Omaha Steak buyers. "People tend to stay with the medium where they first bought," he explains. "We don't generally promote to Web-only buyers with traditional media, although we will continue to test it, especially seasonally. We use a model to determine if and when we're going to mail to you, and the number-one question is 'When did you last buy by mail?' We promote both through Web and mail, but if you only buy via the Web you won't necessarily come out high on the model as a mail buyer. We don't make assumptions if a customer jumps to another medium one time. We don't really do multichannel promotions per se.

Figure 17.1: The Web site at www.omahasteaks.com represents a meat lover's paradise. Omaha Steaks offers exceptional beef, veal, pork, lamb, seafood and kosher foods on the site.

Figure 17.2: Omaha Steaks developed a separate brand and Web site for A La Zing (www.alazing.com) in order to sell full meals as well as pasta, side dishes and desserts.

Figure 17.3: Like the firm's Web site, telemarketing and other selling methods, the Omaha Steaks catalog division represents a separate profit center for the parent company.

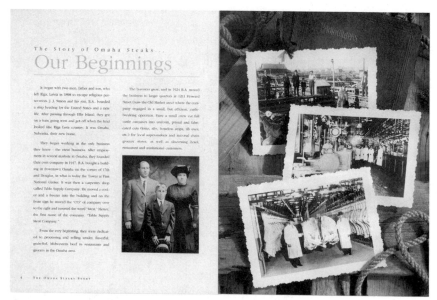

Figure 17.4: J.J. Simon and his son B..A. Simon started Omaha Steaks in 1917 in Omaha, Nebraska after migrating to the United States in 1898. The Simons left Ellis Island and took a train west until they reached Omaha, an area they felt looked much like the farm land in their native Riga, Latvia. The Simon family still owns and runs Omaha Steaks today.

Any cross-channel buying is considered a bonus. We don't try to assign a 'Web effect' to a mailing. There's enough temporary migration in both directions that it's kind of a wash."

Each Profit Center Has Its Own Database

Omaha Steaks has a separate customer and transaction database for each medium through which it sells, including mail, phone, retail, Internet and business-to-business. "Those databases can be cross-referenced as necessary," Simon comments, "and the same outside database management company that houses our list, takes care of this for all aspects of the company." Each Omaha Steaks marketing channel is so independent that they must "make a deal" to trade or sell each other names internally, according to Simon. "Since we run each area as a separate profit center, I would have to give my mail order people an incentive to rent their names to the online business."

Even so, the company has embraced Customer Relationship Management so that its buyers enjoy seamless information flow no matter what medium they choose to tap for their next purchase or customer service question. "We have our own system we developed in-house—with a suite of applications our customer reps use that gives consistent info across media," Simon explains. Both marketing and IT staffers at Omaha Steaks keep a constant eye out for learning on the Web site that can help them improve both their Internet business and the functions of other channels as well.

Simon believes that the profit center approach helps emphasize the importance of each marketing channel to the overall success of Omaha Steaks:

> Our mail order business, our call center, our retail stores, our B-to-B area and our Internet business are all critical to our success and are multiple tentacles on the same product line. Our online channel has become more significant, and we have made an effort to integrate Web sites with retail, with food service, and with our incentive business.
>
> We also are using the Web as an important communication tool. You can track your order online no matter where you ordered; we can use e-mail to keep you informed even if you called in. We maximize the communication aspect of the Internet throughout our business. It has revolutionized our ability to use e-mail, transmit catalog files and pages and much more. It's an important business tool as well as a sales channel.

Building for the Future with A La Zing

Omaha Steaks is taking a similar studied approach to its newest on-line venture, a site called A La Zing (www.alazing.com). Simon and his colleagues wanted to tap into the lucrative market for prepared individual and family meals, but consumer research showed that they would do better marketing such a line under a different name. "That's because of the 'steaks-only' reputation of Omaha Steaks," Simon explains. With 22 complete meals originally online and more options coming, A La Zing offers busy consumers the chance to stock gourmet meals in their freezers. The food can be prepared quickly in the microwave or oven-baked.

A La Zing customers and prospects receive tempting e-mail offers with click-through to HTML images. Everything from a simple weekday meal for two to a Thanksgiving, Christmas or Easter feast can be selected and received in a few days' time via UPS.

Because the Omaha Steaks online business has been tracked as a separate profit center since Day One, Simon knows it

> . . . has been in the black since the beginning. That's because we didn't over-invest. We grew slowly and didn't lose money. The key is to keep the investment in line with a reasonable expectation on return. We know how much we can spend to build a retail store; we know how much we can spend to build the Web site and still make money.
>
> Over time we have goosed up our level of investment commensurate with revenue. We think our Internet business is incremental to Omaha Steaks because of this new channel and tapping into a new demographic—younger and more affluent. But no matter what the medium, the same basics always apply. It's not Internet retailing, it's retailing . . . on the Internet. You need to ship your product promptly, provide good user experience, and top service. It's the great retailers who will win out online.

Chapter Recap:

- Omaha Steaks got online early (1991) and built its online business organically and inexpensively.
- Each Omaha Steaks channel attracts a distinctly different customer base, yet the brand is integrated across all channels.
- Each Omaha Steaks profit center has its own database, yet customers enjoy a seamless flow of information across all channels.
- The introduction of www.alazing.com lets Omaha Steaks diversify into prepared individual and family meals with a new Web site and brand.
- Per Todd Simon of Omaha Steaks: "It's not Internet retailing, it's retailing on the Internet." Good retailers will prevail online as they do in other media.

18 Peapod: Leveraging Logistics
www.peapod.com

If you spend much time in Chicago, Boston, Washington, D.C. or the suburbs of New York City, you've probably spotted at least one VW Bug decorated to resemble a plump green peapod. Those "rolling logos" represent Peapod SVP/Chief Technology Officer Thomas Parkinson's favorite viral marketing method. Parkinson, who founded Peapod in 1989 with his brother Andrew, drives one of the bugs to and from work and has been known to appear in a bright green peapod costume on corporate occasions.

Early in his career, Andrew Parkinson worked at Domino's Pizza as a delivery driver. There he learned his initial lessons in logistics—and later joined forces with Thomas to launch one of America's first online grocery delivery services. In the early days, the Peapod business model was simple. Customers called or went online using Peapod software to order their groceries. Andrew, Thomas and their

Figure 18.1: The clean lines of the Peapod home page at www.peapod.com draw attention to the smiling delivery person—one of Peapod's most important assets in its relationship with customers.

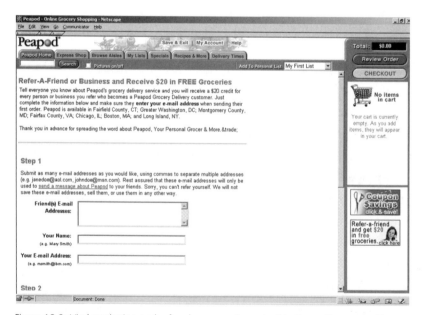

Figure 18.2: Viral marketing and referrals are very important to Peapod's success. Here on the Web page, customers are invited to refer friends and neighbors to the firm. Customers receive $20 for each referral who becomes a Peapod grocery delivery customer.

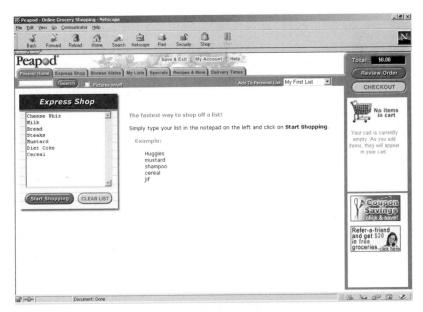

Figure 18.3: The Express Shop feature makes it easy for Peapod customers to choose the items they want and complete an easy transaction.

employees "picked and packed" groceries right off the supermarket shelves and delivered them for a fee. Since then, Peapod has grown to become a leading Internet grocer, and its business model has far surpassed the rudiments of pizza delivery. Now owned by Ahold, the international food retail and food service company based in The Netherlands, Peapod's annual sales are in the $100 million range. The firm represents one of the most sophisticated supply-chain stories in today's online world.

Peapod's "Smart Mile"

At Peapod headquarters in Chicago's northern suburbs resides the firm's unique "Smart Mile Center." There, staffers monitor Peapod delivery loads and routes with the intensity of an air traffic control center or a war room. Half-empty delivery trucks yield the same profitability woes that plague airlines with empty seats and hotels with unused rooms, so Peapod's strategy is to push real-time incentives toward customers on the routes where it needs to fill trucks.

"We don't want every customer," says Mike Brennan, Peapod's SVP/Product Management and Marketing. Brennan's experience with FedEx and UPS prepared him to help perfect the delivery and incentive systems at Peapod. "We only want the profitable customers that are on our route, producing sizeable orders. We look at orders per route per zip code per day. If a customer goes online and we need to fill their route, they see incentives." This is all done within each 24-hour period to ensure timely deliveries. Peapod's average order contains 35 items for a total sale of $130.

Thomas Parkinson, who worked directly with Brennan to develop the "smart mile" system, adds, "You can either manage supply or manage demand. We don't take supply away; we move demand around. This system has helped increase our sales because before, people couldn't get the delivery times they wanted, and didn't see any reason to compromise. We saw a 50 percent increase in orders per truck by incentivizing people to accept certain times for delivery."

Parkinson notes, "We use pricing as another lever to increase basket size. Customers pay a different fee based on order size. For current customers we have a Weekly Specials e-mail that about 65 percent of our customers sign up to receive." Offers can be personalized as well, based on actual buying and/or e-mail subscriptions to various categories. Customers also can ask to be alerted via e-mail when their favorite brands are on sale.

Peapod's Personal Touch

Peapod executives admit that finding managers and delivery drivers to implement their system is vital and sometimes challenging. "We have trouble getting logistics people who can deal with a 'consumer-friendly driver' as opposed to an on-the-road trucker," Brennan says. "The driver is the only person the customer sees. They often develop a real bond with that driver."

Parkinson adds, "We're looking for salespeople who can drive, not drivers who can just carry stuff. We want to be a frictionless experience for customers—like when you go to Starbucks. 'Sure, I'll pay a delivery fee.' It's about not having to deal with hassles in this part of your life anymore." Peapod drivers go through training in operations, paperwork, talking to customers, and how to work with people at their homes. Background checks on drivers help ensure safety for customers and manage risk for Peapod.

Community involvement helps provide positive buzz for Peapod. Like brick-and-mortar grocery chains, Peapod is heavily involved in school programs and fundraisers. This helps encourage word of mouth, which both Brennan and Parkinson find "powerful and affordable." If customers can answer questions about Peapod for prospective customers, the path to an initial sale is beautifully paved. As Brennan notes, "Everyone has the same five or six questions about Peapod. 'Do you accept coupons? How fresh is the food? How reliable is the delivery,' and so on.

Every Peapod employee—right up to the CEO and SVPs—has personal business cards with an individual referral code on the back, too. When a new customer uses that code for a first order the employee gets a financial reward—just another way to emphasize the personal, "viral marketing" culture.

Wanted: Creative Logistics Managers— and Much, Much More

Finding the right operations people is difficult for Peapod because the firm is so fast moving and innovative. Parkinson explains, "We are breaking new ground with some of these concepts and we need managers who can innovate and implement."

Keeping up with customer route demand has been challenging as well. Parkinson recalls, "We used to do 11 to 12 orders per route, then took what we thought was a big plunge to get trucks that could hold 18 orders. We thought we'd never get past that size, but now we find it's too small, and our leases are relatively long-term."

Through sometimes-painful experience, Peapod executives have grown a business that continues to thrive while many other Internet grocers have failed. Thomas Parkinson admits that if he were starting from scratch today, he would launch a very different kind of online business in a different industry entirely. "I would make sure there is a wide margin for profitability from the first month," he insists. "A low-margin business like groceries is tough. The barriers to entry are huge in this industry. It's hard to work to build an infrastructure."

That's one big reason why firms like Webvan and ShopLink failed: They tried to build their own warehouses right away instead of working in tandem with existing "bricks and mortar" grocery store chains. Peapod officials now believe they have "critical mass" in Chicago to build their own warehouse there. Previously it would have been cost-ineffective to do so. Indeed, Peapod CEO Marc van Gelder calls Peapod "the first true clicks-and-mortar success story" for its early alliance with Jewel Foods in Chicago. Today, Peapod works in tandem with bricks and mortar retailers owned by Ahold to deliver its products and services.

Parkinson says that in theory, the Webvan/ShopLink model is superior to Peapod's, but in today's world it hasn't proven practical. As Brennan adds, "There are certain forces of why a business works—it's 'business physics.' How people shop, what's feasible, selling to them at a distance. You have to figure out how to link the old way of buying with something new that customers want. We're focusing on the slice of people who want to shop quickly with a limited number of products. We are a transaction site. Our customers don't want to chat and read. We help them shop fast and smart. We'll sort by unit price, fat content, whatever is important to them. They can click 'previous order' so they don't have to create a list each time. They don't want to pick it up at the store; they want delivery. Grocery is a $400 billion business in the U.S.; we'll be happy with $5 billion of it." With online grocery shopping predicted to grow to $8.8 billion by 2004 according to the researchers at International Data Corp.—and roughly doubling every year since 1999—Peapod has a prime opportunity to pursue that goal in the years to come.

Chapter Recap:

- Peapod's "Smart Mile" concept involves monitoring and shaping delivery loads and routes to maximize profits through targeted and timely customer incentives.
- Peapod's delivery drivers provide a personal touch: They are chosen for their sales personalities first; ability as a driver comes second.
- Community involvement, viral marketing and an aggressive referral program are all parts of Peapod's success formula.
- Synergy with a bricks-and-mortar partner makes the online grocery business practical for Peapod where independents such as Webvan have failed.

19 Quixtar: Ditto Delivery
www.quixtar.com

Like the clear-eyed child who exposed "the Emperor's New Clothes" as a sham, Quixtar Managing Director Ken McDonald enjoys serving as a cyberspace truth-teller. Visit him for a chat and the first words out of his mouth dispel some of the most insidious myths about the Internet. "The Web isn't a miracle, it isn't easy, and customers are fickle. It's not as cheap to go online as people thought it would be, and it doesn't replace print!"

McDonald and his staff are remarkably candid about the fortunes and foibles of Quixtar, a thriving young dot.com with an impressive pedigree. The parent company of this well-funded start-up is Alticor, which also numbers the famous multilevel marketer Amway among its corporate holdings. And while Quixtar resides in a separate building a mile or so from Alticor's world headquarters, it boasts a powerful inheritance: complete access to the database of hundreds of thousands of Amway Independent Business Owners (IBOs) throughout the United States and Canada. Another sister company, Access Business Group, provides Quixtar with manufacturing and distribution.

Quixtar has cannibalized the traditional Amway business on purpose, according to Alticor and Quixtar executives. This Web-based business is seen as the wave of the future for Alticor in the United States and Canada. But that's only part of the story. Today as many as 80 percent of Quixtar IBOs were never in the Amway business. They've discovered Quixtar through other IBOs and word of mouth.

When Quixtar went online for the first time on 9/1/99, IBOs and their friends and families hovered over their computers in breathless anticipation, ready to log on at the appointed moment. They'd been hearing about this new opportunity for months already, and they wanted to be among the first to see Quixtar go live. The result? Quixtar attracted 20 million hits that very day, far more than they'd ever dreamed possible. Unfortunately, the site's "gate" was too small to accommodate the number of visitors, so most visitors got the equivalent of an online busy signal.

"We had to get up to the capacity our IBOs and their customers needed, and we had to do it fast," McDonald recalls. "We learned a lot about technical architecture and rebuilt our site in that first 30 days—separating content servers from transactional servers. We learned on the fly that one big server doesn't work. What we needed to protect and isolate was the transaction material." McDonald and his staff put out a nationwide all-points bulletin for a certain type of Compaq server and sent trucks out to get them. He adds, "Our original door was only so big. It didn't take us long to figure out that we needed a whole lot bigger door."

Figure 19.1: The Quixtar home page (www.quixtar.com) shows an array of products available to customers through their Independent Business Owners (IBOs). These include cleaning products, food, health and beauty aids, lawn and garden products and much more.

Figure 19.2: Quixtar is the largest health and beauty site in the online world today. This page shows an array of the firm's food supplements, diet products, vitamins and herbs.

Figure 19.3: The *Choices* and *Store for More*™ catalogs have become a vital part of Quixtar's marketing and communications mix. The firm began its life without a print presence but quickly realized that integration of online and offline media would be necessary for optimum success.

Product + Platform =
Online Entrepreneurial Opportunity

Whereas some pundits position Quixtar simply as an eMall, a health-and-beauty site, or a business opportunity, the firm's Media Team Leader Robin Luymes says, "We are all of those things, as well as being the largest health-and-beauty e-commerce site." Vice-President of Sales and Marketing John Parker adds, "We are still trying to figure out what our industry is. I think our biggest competitor on the Internet is eBay because it provides a platform for individuals to have their own businesses. We provide the product *and* the platform whereas eBay provides the platform only." McDonald adds, "We provide a whole turnkey business. We are somewhere between eBay and a more traditional direct marketing firm."

He continues, "Rather than trying to morph Amway into some type of online business, we've taken a different tack. We chose to create a completely new business, a sister company that operates in different ways and provides different features and benefits to capitalize on entrepreneurship and the lure of the Web—and the opportunity it presents to provide a turnkey operation simply and inexpensively."

John Parker explains this concept in greater detail: "The relationship we have with our Access Business Group sister company provides the basic foundation of Quixtar's business. Unlike a pure start-up like Webvan, we already had the kind of expertise we needed in-house. Access provides us with manufacturing and distribution. Well-known branded products like Artistry (cosmetics), Nutrilite (nutritional items) and LOC (cleaning supplies), are made by Access. They have warehouses and distribution centers throughout the United States and Canada. They ensure that we can make good on our promise to IBOs that products will be delivered right to their customers' doors. Where a pure dot.com could only show you a room full of servers and other 'tech stuff,' we can give you a tour of our warehouse operation."

In addition to the Access brands, Quixtar offers IBOs the opportunity to increase their sales and diversity of offerings through relationships with a host of top-notch affiliates with "stores" on the Quixtar site. "There are hundreds and thousands of products available on Quixtar that are not available from Amway," John Parker says. Quixtar holds these partners to exceedingly high standards of product quality and back-end sophistication. Each partner needs to be able to not only deliver effectively to Quixtar customers but also to report back sales at the individual IBO level for proper credit toward performance bonuses.

The payoff for partners can be enormous: Quixtar reports that it represents either the number-one or number-two such relationship for many of the partner stores (affiliates) that appear on its site. Among the partners listed in a recent check of the site are many big names among retailers, catalogers and dot.coms including True Value Hardware, Magellan's, Omaha Steaks, DisneyStore.com, KBToys.com, and OfficeMax.com.

A Blend of High Tech with High Touch

While Quixtar IBOs fit into a hierarchy that has some similarities to classic multilevel marketing, their rewards are more direct than those of the traditional Amway system. Every customer who purchases even a tube of toothpaste on the Quixtar site must enter an IBO's number to place an order. New customers who do not have an IBO can be linked with one via e-mail—typically in just a day or so.

Ideally, McDonald and Parker envision each IBO and customer interacting in a neighborly way—"over the back fence" as they put it. The IBO helps the customer identify Quixtar products that fulfill their needs, then encourages or even helps the customer go online to order. Products are delivered direct to the customer's door—the IBO does not have to take them into inventory. IBOs are paid by means of "performance bonuses." Their bonuses also positively impact payments to their "upline"—the IBO who got them involved and perhaps one or any number of layers above that.

Quixtar's Biggest Coup: Ditto Delivery

The power of the IBO's relationship with the individual customer becomes clear in an examination of Quixtar's biggest success to date: a "ship 'til forbid" program called Ditto Delivery. As John Parker notes, "Ditto Delivery is an automatic replenishment plan for consumable products like diapers, vitamins, dog food, toothpaste and shampoo. Our customers can cross those items off their supermarket shopping lists for good, and have them shipped to their door monthly, every-other month or however often they choose. Because the customer fills out the profile just once and then can forget it, this program delivers on the Web's elusive promise of saving time and making life easier." Ditto Delivery already represents between 25 and 30 percent of Quixtar's overall sales.

The overwhelming success of Ditto Delivery came as a surprise to McDonald and Parker, but they now understand why the program has become so powerful. Left to their own devices, customers would be unlikely to sit down and methodically set up their own Ditto Delivery web profiles. But when their IBO encourages them, explains the benefits of the program and sits beside them to talk them through the form, the completion rate skyrockets. Ditto Delivery is a true "win-win" situation. It relieves customers of a good part of their shopping burden, and at the same time provides IBOs with a dependable and lucrative backlog of business.

Empowering IBOs is Job One for Quixtar

John Parker admits that Quixtar executives originally envisioned creating "the world's greatest shopping site." He now says that vision has changed to "the infrastructure for an IBO's business—but still satisfying for the individual." In terms of Customer Relationship Management, leveraging the IBOs' power and their personal touch is crucial. As Parker notes, "With our IBOs, we have a couple hundred thousand touchpoints out there. It's person-to-person, referral-based marketing." Quixtar paid $146 million in bonuses and incentives in its first year of online business. McDonald provides a frame of reference: "We paid out almost as much in bonuses and incentives our first year as Amazon.com had in sales its first year!"

Learning on the fly and providing what IBOs and customers need keeps Quixtar executives hopping, and they pride themselves on being able to switch directions quickly. One year they cut distribution of their paper Christmas book in half, with dire results. McDonald says, "We learned the print versus online lesson sooner than Lands' End. We realized very early on that we couldn't ignore print." Parker adds that Quixtar customers "shop offline and buy online"—so the slick, colorful catalogs that Quixtar produces are essential to maximizing sales.

McDonald says that IBOs have appreciated the increasing levels of personalization available to them and their customers on the Quixtar site. The firm also provides support to IBOs in developing, enhancing and maintaining their own customer databases. "Rather than just one big front door or one big store, you see one thing if you are an IBO, another as a member, another as a client. As an IBO you can customize the front page for your volume targets and your volume. We deliver what is relevant to their business. IBOs tell us what they want to see."

One thing that the IBOs and Quixtar customers did *not* want to see was MyQuixtar—something, VP-Chief Information Officer (CIO) Randy Bancino says, "we dreamed up on the same day as Ditto Delivery." MyQuixtar was a personalized portal with news feeds, personalized weather, horoscopes and the like. "It never took off," Bancino notes, "because people prefer the Yahoos and the AOLs of the world. We weren't adding any significant value in that space, so we killed it." Bancino says that IBOs and customers have also nixed site features "that are just plain cute. They get a big spike and then usage just plummets." These now-abandoned features include personalized faces for trying make-up and building a table with dinnerware patterns of your choice. Bancino adds, "We have been diligent about looking at every feature and function"—and eliminating anything that doesn't meet IBO and customer expectations."

Chapter Recap:

- Quixtar has cannibalized the traditional Amway direct selling business on purpose and is seen as the wave of the future by Alticor, the parent company of both firms.
- Combining Amway's traditional products with a wide new assortment of additional products and an exceptional online platform provides a unique entrepreneurial opportunity for Quixtar's Independent Business Owners.
- Quixtar strives for a combination of online high tech with IBOs' high touch.
- Ditto Delivery (a ship'til forbid program) represents Quixtar's biggest success to date.
- Quixtar's main goal for its site and programs is to empower its IBOs to serve their customers better.

20 | Spiegel:
Small Staff/Big Results
www.spiegel.com

"The brand is the number-one factor in our success with Spiegel on-line," says Rich Burke, Spiegel's Divisional Vice-President, Spiegel I-Media. "Fifty percent of the people who visit our Web site key in www.spiegel.com," Burke adds, an indication that many visitors already know the Spiegel name and don't need to find the site through a search engine, banner or affiliate link.

"Our second strength online stems from Spiegel's established fulfillment and customer service areas," Burke continues. "As far as the rest of the e-commerce industry, it's pretty much the same. The real winners to date are the catalogers who already had the brand, infrastructure and fulfillment in place before they went online. With just 15 people in Spiegel's e-commerce division, we did over $150 million in sales during 2001 because we leveraged everything else in the company."

Figure 20.1: Attractive pictures representing the various product categories at www.spiegel.com lead customers into their online shopping experience.

Figure 20.2: While Spiegel has been careful to avoid nonproduct content that distracts customers from buying, the firm has found horoscopes to be very popular with its customers—and products on horoscope pages often register outstanding sales.

Figure 20.3: The Spiegel catalog puts the www.spiegel.com Web site in front of prospects and customers 120 million times each year. The strength of the catalog brand has been key to the Web site's success.

Burke leads a Spiegel marketing department team that is 100 percent focused on the Internet:

> These 15 people execute what needs to be done for the Web site, but they're also charged with liaison work into Spiegel's 'silo groups' to harness their strength as much as we can. With 15 staffers we can really benefit from the work of 300. That's been a big win and has overcome difficulty. Another way we leverage is through our sister companies, Eddie Bauer and Newport News. As a large player on the Web we negotiate decent pricing for everything from advertising agencies to banner ads, Web development and portal deals.

The growth of Spiegel's Internet sales is even more significant for the company in that the firm attracts a slightly younger customer online. This bodes well for long-term customer value. What's more, Burke notes, "Internet customers account for a high percentage of the new Spiegel customers, period."

Speed Bumps on Spiegel's Internet Highway

Burke does not want to imply that Spiegel has embraced Internet marketing without problems or delays:

> The initial thought was that e-commerce was going to be an inexpensive way to get customers and sell product, but we've found it's not inexpensive at all. The other misperception is how fast you can move online. But the more complicated our site becomes, we find it almost takes an act of God to get it changed. We have a big priority list and we're always re-prioritizing. Overall it's nowhere near as inexpensive or easy as we once thought to get things done online.

The traditional Spiegel catalog culture has presented some stumbling blocks as well. However, as Burke notes:

> In a company of this size, when a priority is put on something like the Internet, it's kind of like 'the skids are greased.' You can't do much without IT assistance, but management is behind it, so IT gets that message. Some people here still don't get it, though. They are concerned about the Web site's cannibalization or robbing from other channels.
>
> The bigger the Internet section of marketing becomes, the more some catalog people seem concerned about losing power. The catalog is not growing in revenue these days, but the Internet is. Perhaps the real problem is that if certain employees don't know much about the Internet area, its growth is threatening to them. The same is true with our merchandising people. They're learning about how things work on the 'Net. Our CEO has been saying, 'Don't worry about what channel customers buy from as long as they buy,' but people in specific catalog disciplines still worry about it.

He adds: that one of his goals is to help veteran Spiegel employees gain a higher level of comfort with the Internet.

One way to do that is to make sure fellow employees realize that the traditional business is what allows the Spiegel Web site to thrive. "The catalog is so key—120 million times a year we get www.spiegel.com in front of people when that catalog arrives. The Internet will provide more than 20 percent of corporate profit on about 15 percent of the sales this year, but if we didn't have the catalog and the brand, our site would be ho-hum.

"Our site is highly supported by the catalog business. We don't see that changing. Even so, new customers, sales and profitability are coming from the Internet. We are now a multichannel company, which is very positive. Our retail clearance outlets are becoming less important, however, because we can use the Internet for clearance. We outsell bluefly.com five times with our outlet site, www.ultima-teoutlet.com."

Don't Let Content and Community Hamper Sales

Burke is a pragmatist about the Internet, dubbing it "High-speed direct marketing. Not different than the past 135 years. The delivery vehicle is a little different, though. There are some things about the Internet that makes it impractical to just put your catalog online. People expect the 'Net to be more fun, they want interactivity, and they won't tolerate back orders online. They expect better service, and they don't want to talk to people—you have to make it easy for them to transact without talking to anyone. Our most important vendor is the company that hosts our Web site. If it runs slow and people don't come back, we may have lost them for good."

Spiegel debuted its first Web site in 1995 with "pure content," according to Burke. It was what he calls an "image test site." When the site's purpose changed to e-commerce in the fourth quarter of 1997, Spiegel staged a relaunch that eliminated all nonselling content.

It was not until the fall of 2001 that Burke began testing relevant content on the site to "support the e-commerce piece and increase stickiness." The rationale for testing more content stems from Spiegel's success with horoscopes on the site. "Women love horoscopes," he observes. "Conversion is seven times higher when we push product through horoscopes." The content tests include topics such as women's health, family issues and styling tips for the home. So far the content is kept separate from the main selling areas of the site so it doesn't provide roadblocks for shoppers who want to get on and get off quickly.

"I don't want you to have to stay there very long to buy," Burke says of the Spiegel Web site. "You can stay online and do a lot if you want, but we want to facilitate quick buying. Our peak times are 1 p.m. and late at night. Women who are buying at work want to do it fast. I want to make shopping with us as smooth and easy and non-obtrusive on her life as I can but also want to offer extra opportunities like virtual fashion shows. As for building community on the site, I don't believe it's relevant. With kids or seniors it might make sense but for our average busy Spiegel customer, no."

Burke is also not in a hurry to add much customization or personalization to the Spiegel site. "We're not at all planning to do the amazon.com thing with personalization," he says. "I don't really want to be addressed as 'Hi, Rich.' I'm still searching for a company that says, 'We wouldn't be here today if it weren't for personalization.'

"Personalization makes the most sense to me on e-mail," he counters. "Ours goes out 'one to a few' instead of 'one to many,' based on your actual buying history rather than what some computer thinks you might buy. We will do 58 million e-mails this year, and are just starting to focus on segmentation. E-mail is our lowest cost-per-action advertising vehicle."

Rather than spend large amounts of money on personalization or CRM software, Burke believes in heavying up the investment in fulfillment. "If you over-deliver on fulfillment, what better CRM is there than that? I don't believe in building in so much on the front end. I think it's better to provide better quality and packaging than expected on the customer's doorstep. I'm not big on bells and whistles. Customers will forgive you for no bells and whistles on the site, but will not forgive slow-loading sites and packages that don't show up. We have stuck to blocking and tackling."

That being said, Burke does offer his customers some helpful site features that increase order size in the bargain. "We'll show you a dress and then offer accessories that go well with it. Also, after your order is finished online we'll say, 'How about adding this on for $9.95. That is customized by past buying.'"

A Multifaceted Approach
to Acquisition and Retention

In terms of attracting new customers via www.spiegel.com, Burke has enjoyed Spiegel's success with affiliate programs, and has ties with about 350 affiliates that send traffic to his site. On the other hand, Spiegel has only a handful of affiliate links outgoing from its site. "When we send people traffic we try to pick only firms that will enhance our brand," he explains. As for reciprocal links, Burke is not an advocate. "I don't know why I would send somebody elsewhere. On our thank-you page we have a couple of links where we send people, mostly Spiegel partners that pay us a commission." Spiegel also does considerable banner advertising, drawing on the knowledge of its catalog database experts to help target sites with highest potential.

As for acquisition, Burke is working on maximizing revenues from customers who buy on the Internet and/or via catalog. "If you buy on the Web but have never bought via catalog, we circulate you very heavily. We also circulate Web offers to catalog-only buyers, but that has been less than successful. Internet shoppers are very willing to shop the catalog but not vice-versa and we haven't yet determined why. If we can get them to buy through both media, our records show that their value to us doubles. We try not to make the choice for the customer on channel—buy however you want to buy. If we advertise a promotion in the catalog it can be redeemed on the 'Net and vice-versa."

Going forward, Burke believes his direct marketing mindset will serve www.spiegel.com well. "We test everything. It's the catalog mentality. We don't do anything without a test. We use control groups and standard testing methods—the same things we have done for years in direct mail. A typical e-mail test pits six different creative pitches against each other. We don't test price but we do test promotions, layouts, heading changes and category changes. Every word on the site has been tested one way or the other."

Chapter Recap:

- Spiegel's online success can be traced to the firm's strong brand as well as its established fulfillment and customer service infrastructures.
- Just 15 people with 100 percent focus on the Internet are able to serve as liaisons to Spiegel's "silo groups" and leverage online marketing and sales.
- For Spiegel, content and community-building aspects are less important than sales.
- More than 350 affiliates help drive traffic to the Spiegel Web site.
- The catalog also is a key driver, putting the www.spiegel.com URL in front of customers and prospects 120 million times per year.
- Integrating online and offline media are keys to maximizing Spiegel's acquisition and retention efforts.
- Spiegel tests everything it can online including, promotions, layouts, headings and categories.

21 | Steelcase:
The Power of Ensync
www.steelcase.com

With wireless Internet access and high-tech trappings throughout its open-plan offices, the Steelcase eTools Group makes an ideal showcase for the company's architecture, furniture and technology products. While the rest of Steelcase headquarters emits an air of polished formality, the eTools area features a live satellite feed along with a Lucite surfboard-shaped table in the entry area, concrete floors, flexible furniture products and plush casual seating in bright colors.

According to Jeff Vredevoogd, Manager, eTools Marketing for Steelcase, this office environment is all part of the Steelcase online culture. "Our goal as a company is to help people work more effectively—wherever, whenever and however they work. The Internet helps us push the envelope of possibilities," he explains.

Steelcase has been leveraging the Internet for many years,

launching its first customer e-business effort including on-line transactions and system integration in 1995. Since then, Steelcase has been able to develop "a comprehensive, integrated solution" made possible by the development of user-centered eTools designed to perform by themselves or in combination with other tools.

A key element of Steelcase's eTools offering is Ensync™, the company's proprietary B2B software platform. Ensync is the customer's Web portal for accessing information or conducting transactions with Steelcase and Steelcase dealers.

Vredevoogd firmly believes the Steelcase online presence to be far superior to that of Steelcase's competitors. "Our focus is much broader. A broad vision drives broad solutions, and that leads to broad value for our customers."

Comprehensive, Integrated Solutions

Today, Steelcase's goal is to leverage the Internet in order to strengthen customer relationships by providing them with a comprehensive, integrated solution that can support them through the facilities management process. Steelcase's "eCapabilities" serve the customer in many ways—from managing information and visualizing potential solutions for their office environment to simplifying the process of obtaining products and services and managing existing furniture assets more effectively.

"Ensync provides the customer with a totally customizable shopping experience. It provides customer-specific product and service catalogs tailored to the customer's existing products, pricing and processes. In addition, it mirrors the customer's approval process by routing orders automatically to the appropriate decision maker(s). In the end, it saves the customer time and money," says Vredevoogd.

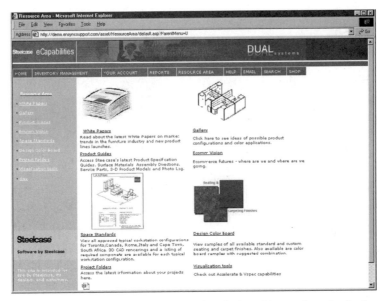

Figure 21.1: Steelcase "eCapabilities" as described on this page from the firm's Web site include white papers, product guides, project folders, design color boards and visualization tools.

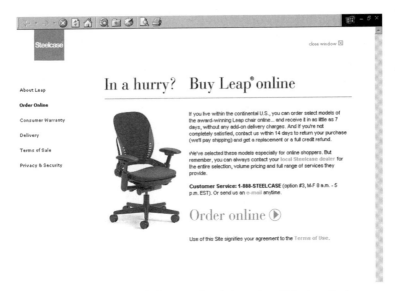

Figure 21.2: While some might have predicted channel conflict when Steelcase began selling its famous Leap chair at www.steelcase.com, the firm's dealers have been pleased by the move. Why? Most prospects who ask to purchase more than five Leap chairs are referred directly to their closest Steelcase dealer.

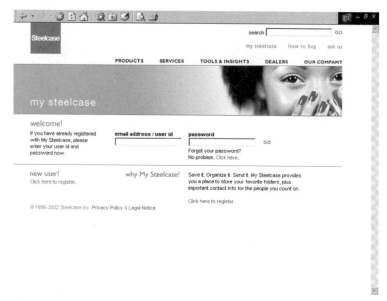

Figure 21.3: MySteelcase allows customers to save their plans, organize their work and share design ideas with co-workers as well as their Steelcase dealer.

But today, instead of commerce being the primary focus, it has become one of many eCapabilities that Steelcase offers. "It's no longer acceptable to offer just a shopping cart. Customers expect much more, you have to be able to deliver," Vredevoogd continues. He adds:

> While having a shopping cart can respond to specific customer needs, Steelcase's advantage is its ability to help customers save time through the easy access and management of information. This information can take on many faces: order-related information (both on-line orders and orders placed directly with their Steelcase dealer), company-specific information, project-related information, etc. These capabilities exist within Ensync.

A key feature of Ensync is the Resource Area. This customizable area provides the customer with a single place to access key information as well as a place for online collaboration—with their Steelcase dealer, with each other, etc. An example of this is the ability for a customer to view possible office design options quickly. Within the Resource Area customers can view their online office furniture standards, approved material palettes, installation photos, CAD drawings, etc. The customer can view and compare options that are available to them as well as share project files and drawings with their dealer.

Finally, Steelcase solutions help customers improve and simplify the management of existing furniture assets. "Customers appreciate the fact that Ensync provides the option to order something new, or pull from existing inventory that is managed by their Steelcase dealer—all on line," says Vredevoogd. "Customers save a great deal of money by reusing products they already own. Steelcase makes this possible."

"This is a good example of how integration can help our customers. Ensync integrates with SnapTracker (Steelcase's asset management software) to make this possible. Customers are not required to step out of one tool to get to another with different passwords. We look to Ensync as the customer's view in—a single front door, so to speak"

Vredevoogd adds, "Steelcase will continue to focus on expanding its eCapabilities. By working with customers and our dealers, we recognize there are still many opportunities worthy of consideration."

Partnering with Dealers to Meet Customer Needs

The Internet has not changed Steelcase's relationship with its dealers, according to Vredevoogd. "The Steelcase dealer network represents the strongest channel in the industry. They are envied by their peers, they provide local level support, and Steelcase couldn't exist without them. We're proud to be partners with them."

Steelcase works closely with its dealers to create customer-specific solutions. While the eTools team may lead the development and marketing efforts for Steelcase eTools, it is often the local Steelcase dealer who positions or tailors the specific solution for the client, ensuring that the customers needs are met with a comprehensive, integrated solution.

Dealers also are establishing their own presence on the 'Net. How deeply they go in developing their own site is up to them— from using the Internet as simply a marketing tool on one end to becoming a one-stop source for everything related to their business with their customers and their partners.

Vredevoogd shares that www.steelcase.com, Steelcase's public Web site, is experimenting with selling direct to consumers, but even these experiments are done with dealer approval in mind. The www.steelcase.com site features one of Steelcase's most renowned products, the ergonomically advanced Leap, chair, on its face. There's a click-through area for "Order Leap Now," where Web site visitors can select a chair or two for direct delivery by FedEx.

If the customer expresses interest in more than five Leap chairs, they're notified that they could save money on that larger purchase by working with a Steelcase dealer. The customer can then be linked to a Steelcase dealer in their area who can facilitate the transaction.

Serving Customers Better . . . And Saving Time and Money Online

The power of Ensync is its ability to be tailored to the needs of the user, providing easy access to information, on-line ordering, project files, etc. This all adds up to time and money savings.

"Steelcase is primarily concerned with the user. We focus on them, providing easy access to the information they need in a format that works for them. Providing the customer with opportunities to customize their view into our solutions helps make their experience more valuable and enjoyable," says Vredevoogd.

Another example of how Steelcase tailors its solutions to the customer is its public website (www.steelcase.com). A new feature is mysteelcase, which gives the visitor the ability to select information that is important to them and places it in a personalized folder. This folder is available every time the user signs on providing quick and easy access to the preselected information. In addition, it also provides the ability to share the contents of the personalized folder with others via email.

"Customers typically look to the manufacturer as the primary source for product information and a growing number are coming to the Web to research products early in the buying process. Visitors come to our site from all over the world. Our goal is to make it easy for them to find what they are looking for and organize it for future visits in the way that works best for them," says Eileen Raphael, Manager, www.steelcase.com. In conclusion, Vredevoogd notes that Steelcase will continue to focus on providing a complete solution for its customers and dealers. "A comprehensive, integrated solution" is his goal for the eTools Group:

> Our focus is not just to streamline the purchase of a new chair—we can do that today. Our goal is to streamline, simplify and support our customers through their *entire facility management process*. We will continue to develop tools that will add more value in areas like collaboration and project management. Ultimately, our goal is to serve our customers in ways they never thought possible.

Chapter Recap:

- Steelcase's eTools Group provides "a comprehensive, integrated solution" online for its dealers' use in serving their customers.
- The eTools Group works to leverage the Internet and strengthen customer relations while it supports the total facility management process.
- Customers use eTools for collaboration and project management and also to manage their existing furniture inventories online.
- The www.steelcase.com site now offers the famous Leap chair direct to consumers, but Steelcase avoids conflict with its dealers by referring prospects seeking five or more chairs to their nearest dealer.

22 Yamaha Band & Orchestral Division: Online/Offline Integration
www.yamahaadvantage.com

"Yamaha is one of the top 30 most recognizable brands in the world," says Glenda Plummer, Senior Marketing Manager of Yamaha's Band & Orchestral Division. "The Yamaha corporate Web page (www.yamaha.com) gets over two million hits per month in great part due to the strength of that name. The Salt Lake City Olympics asked us to be their exclusive band instrument provider— they couldn't imagine anybody else doing it. Yet ironically, until recently many of our U.S.-based dealers had completely lost interest in leveraging the strength of the Yamaha name."

Plummer says that at one time Yamaha's dealers actively marketed for the firm, proudly promoting the fact that they carried the Yamaha brand, but in recent years they had stopped. "They marketed themselves and their stores, but not Yamaha. They'd actually un-package Yamaha products and put them in packages with their own store name! Thus for at least part of our activities, we decided we'd have to go around the dealers and market directly to teachers, parents and students, even though we sell exclusively through dealers. Our dealers had become passive middlemen. Direct mail represented our key marketing channel. We had to drive customers to the dealer to ask for Yamaha and nothing else. Not to ask for 'a trumpet,' but *this* trumpet, this *specific Yamaha* trumpet."

Gary Winder, a Regional Sales Manager for Yamaha, explains the dealers' concerns in a global context. "In Japan, Yamaha is sold through its own chain of Yamaha Musical Instruments stores. and in independently owned music stores. Delster, American dealers are determined to make sure we don't get that big and have this happen in the United States. The Japanese culture is still evident to our dealers, and they are wary of it. The perception is that the Japanese have all the technology, much further advanced than the Americans. Rather than admiring this, our American dealers are somewhat jealous of it and act accordingly. Their attitude is, 'You've got great products, but we're going to keep you in your place. So that you don't take over, we have to keep American brands firmly in the picture, too.'"

Yamaha Faces Corporate Challenges Online

Today, Plummer and Winder look to the Internet as the "medium of choice" to supplement and perhaps ultimately supplant direct mail as their dominant marketing medium. Yet the Internet has already developed quite a reputation for stirring up channel clashes, as Bob Stone and Ron Jacobs note in *Successful Direct Marketing Methods* (McGraw-Hill, Seventh Edition, 2001). "Channel conflicts can and do exist as the result of implementing an e-commerce strategy," say Stone and Jacobs. "Business-to-business marketers often find their

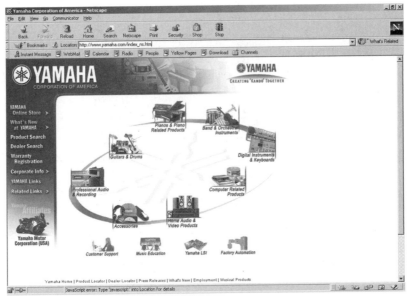

Figure 22.1: The corporate Web site at www.yamaha.com gets over two million hits per month and represents one of the world's 30 most recognized brands. Its contents and look and feel are tightly controlled by the multinational company.

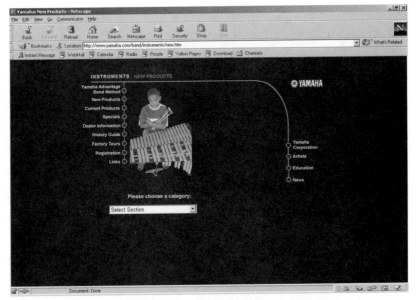

Figure 22.2: From the general Yamaha Web site, visitors can click on a link to this sub-site representing Yamaha Band & Orchestra Division.

Figure 22.3: In order to create a site with more freedom from corporate mandates, Yamaha's Band & Orchestra Division staked out its own URL at www.yamahaadvantage.com. This Web site works in harmony with the Yamaha Advantage book, *Musicianship from Day One*. The Web site has sections for teachers, parents, and music students.

Web presence a challenge to their sales force, their distributors, or other channel partners."

Divisions of an enormous multinational company like Yamaha have some additional frustrations to deal with when attempting to implement their own targeted strategies online. Plummer characterizes the Yamaha site and much else that she sees on the Web as "a huge shotgun blast. You think you can target but you won't necessarily succeed." Plummer also reports that there is a "worldwide corporate push" to be more consistent with the Web sites of Yamaha. That means that most applications are developed slowly and painstakingly, by long-distance and by committee. For example, the Extranet for Yamaha Band & Orchestral Division is being crafted in California, while Plummer and her staff are based in Michigan.

Winder says that the Extranet will be developed in phases and fears it won't be fully implemented until sometime in the future. "The first phase will be strictly look-up. Our salespeople and dealers will be able to get order numbers and track orders. Eventually, dealers will be able to assign different levels of access for their employees so that a salesperson in a store can look up availability, a buyer can place an order, the accountant can look up payment records—all by access codes."

Yamaha Corporate Isn't in a Hurry

Another challenge for Plummer and Winder comes under the category of "good news/bad news." The good news is that their Yamaha division is already way out in front of its major competitors in terms of its online sophistication and offerings. The bad news is that this makes it difficult to free up corporate resources for fast-track online initiatives.

Winder observes, "In the music business generally, we are reluctant to dedicate too many resources or too much time and money to initiatives where we can't be guaranteed an immediate return." Plummer adds, "Most of our competitors are way behind us online, so we don't feel pushed. Some of the smaller firms that are more agile push us a bit, but only in minor areas, like accessories. One of our sister divisions in California—guitars and keyboards—is being pushed by companies like Fender. Dealers are telling us that Fender will take orders for guitars that are customized, then promise an exact delivery date. Even though certain divisions do feel that urgency, Yamaha insists on doing everything as a full corporate initiative."

Overcoming Obstacles to
Marketing Convergence

Despite all these barriers, Yamaha Band & Orchestral Division has launched two successful initiatives that should pave the way for more targeted and personal communications as well as community building directly with teachers, parents, students—and even dealers. The first is the Yamaha Advantage program, and the second is a cooperative direct mail and e-mail program that dealers consider a "win-win" opportunity.

Gary Winder explains, "Our division's biggest online success to date is The Yamaha Advantage™ site at www.yamahaadvantage.com. As you can see, we developed a separate URL for this site rather than trying to integrate it with the restrictive www.yamaha.com site. We outsourced both the print and online materials for this program rather than deal with in-house politics and limitations." The result is an introductory music book and Web site with the same "look and feel," plus a great deal of functionality for music students and teachers alike.

Subtitled "Musicianship from Day One," The Yamaha Advantage book serves as a beginning instrumentalist's guide to everything from care of his or her band instrument to assembly, tuning, making the first sounds, cleaning and storage. The book provides a log for practice times, assignments, teacher goals and student questions. It includes a host of exercises and easy tunes for the beginning instrumentalist, as well as a Certificate of Achievement for the band director to present once the student has completed all the lessons. The book is organized into sections for musicianship, notes, theory and rhythm—all representing three years' worth of input of over 300 band directors who contributed to its creation.

The Web site enriches and enhances The Yamaha Advantage experience for parents, students and teachers alike. They each have their own password-protected areas to visit and learn from. Examples of the online technology include MP3 accompaniments for every song, music theory games and questions and answers with authors Sandy Feldstein and Larry Clark. As Feldstein and Clark assert, "This interactive Web site is designed to help students improve their musicianship and assist teachers in the implementation of this method; but most of all it is designed to be fun!"

As the first band method to create a supplemental online community that enhances the learning experience of students, The Yamaha Advantage represents "value added" for teachers who recommend specific brands and instruments to students. It also builds loyalty on the part of parents and students who find this "best-of-breed" methodology and support system a nearly painless way of getting started in the school band.

Rebuilding a Bridge to Success with Dealer Partners

Gary Winder says that a Yamaha *faux pas* in late 2001 inadvertently led to a major breakthrough in dealer relations. "In December we sent out a direct mail piece that included prices on our products. Some dealers were upset and told us we couldn't dictate pricing that way. I started traveling around to visit complaining dealers and sat down with them to try to develop a compromise. With pressures from the economic downturn, both Yamaha's sales and dealer sales were down, so everyone was looking for a breakthrough."

Winder says that both sides were ready to lay their cards on the table. While Yamaha was willing and able to do its own promotions, the firm found going it alone without dealer cooperation both expensive and "hit or miss." The dealers were still adamant about promoting their own businesses, but they did admit that the Yamaha brand name was a powerful tool. "We agreed that our best path was to work together to leverage the Yamaha brand," Winder explains.

The result was a campaign that began in January 2002, combining direct mail and e-mail in several cooperative efforts. First,

Yamaha leveraged its relationship with Bands of America (www.bands.org) to promote its products in the group's bimonthly HTML newsletter. When responses poured in, Winder used the results to intrigue dealers and offer them a chance to take advantage of the same promotion. Several top dealer organizations in Indiana, New Jersey and Texas stepped up immediately, incentivized with Yamaha co-op advertising money to spread the costs and show corporate support.

According to Winder, it appears that Yamaha and its dealers have finally rediscovered a way to work productively together, using direct mail and e-mail as their platform. As he reports, "In one week, we gained 140,000 impressions for this new promotion through direct and electronic mail. While the incremental cost to Yamaha was less the $10,000, within a matter of days we had booked $3,000,000 in incremental product orders!"

Chapter Recap:

- Yamaha had been using direct mail as the main medium to reach end users since its dealers had become "passive middlemen." It now appears that the Internet can supplement and eventually supplant the firm's direct mail efforts.
- Yamaha represents one of the world's 30 most recognized brands, but its complex corporate environment makes online innovation difficult.
- The Yamaha Advantage music book and Web site represent a pilot campaign for end users with the same "look and feel" throughout and materials aimed at music teachers, parents and students.
- A recent breakthrough for Yamaha indicates that a combination of direct mail and E-mail may help the firm and its dealers to work together productively for the first time in years.

Executives Interviewed for Marketing Convergence

MR. DAVE MARTIN
Chief Financial Officer
Action Performance
Phoenix, Arizona

MR. STEVE KATZMAN
Chief Executive Officer
MR. DAN GILMARTIN
Chief Operating Officer
American Blind & Wallpaper
    Factory
Plymouth, Michigan

MS. DIANA RODRIGUEZ-
    VELAZQUEZ
Director, E-Commerce
    Marketing
Carnival Cruise Lines
Miami, Florida

MR. JIM SHANKS
President, CDW-Government,
    Inc. and Executive
    Vice-President of CDW
Mettawa, IL

MR. KEVIN GIGLINTO
Director of Marketing
Chicago Symphony Orchestra
Chicago, IL

MR. ED BJORNCRANTZ
Former Vice-President of
    Marketing
MR. TIM FORD
President
J. C. Whitney
Chicago, IL

MR. DUNCAN MACLEAN
Former Chief Operating Officer
MS. CATHERINE ETTINGER
Former Chief Executive Officer
MS. JENNIFER JURGENS
Former Marketing Director
MR. JOE FORCE
Former Information Technology
    Director
Mindpepper
Grand Rapids, MI

MR. TODD SIMON
Senior Vice-President
Omaha Steaks
Omaha, Nebraska

MR. MIKE BRENNAN
Senior Vice-President/Product
   Management
MR. THOMAS PARKINSON
Senior Vice-President/Chief
   Technology Officer
Peapod
Skokie, IL

MR. KEN MCDONALD
Managing Director
MR. JOHN PARKER
Vice-President, Sales and
   Marketing
MR. RANDY BANCINO
Vice-President—Chief
   Information Officer
MR. ROBIN LUYMES
Media Team Leader
Quixtar
Ada, MI

MR. RICH BURKE
Divisional Vice-President,
   Spiegel I-Media
Downers Grove, IL

MR. JEFF VREDEVOOGD
Manager, B2B Applications
Steelcase eTools Group
Grand Rapids, MI

MS. GLENDA PLUMMER
Senior Marketing Manager
MR. GARY WINDER
Regional Sales Manager
Yamaha Band and Orchestral
   Division
Kentwood, MI

Index